I0683450

THE ACCIDENTAL SADHU

By

Kim Eugene Hood

ISBN: 979-8-21811672-9

Library of Congress Control Number: 2023901530

Book Design by Kendra Condojani.
Pictures by Kim Eugene Hood.

Printed by IngramSpark, Inc, in the United States of America.

First edition 2024.

Dedication

Dedicated to Tim Hagan. Tim was the closest person to a brother I have ever had. For almost 30 years we climbed mountains, traveled the world, drank whisky and jokingly pursued seven drunks on seven continents. He was an engineer, photographer, pianist and could kick steps up a mountain slope all day long.

Contents

Introduction _____ 1

The Accidental Sadhu _____ 3

*Tibet, A Journey to Mt. Kailash*_____ 7

India and the Four Adobes,
*Travels on the Char Dham*_____ 25

Camino de Santiago,
*Meditation by Feet on the Way of St. James*_____ 67

Conclusion_____ 119

About the Author_____ 121

Introduction

Even though I had visited many sacred sites and had a variety of spiritual experiences through my life, I had never really thought of myself as religious. Being raised in the rural Midwest, it was normal for a child to be baptized, which I was at the age of 12. Baptism of the old-school variety – white robed, underwater immersion. As a young adult in the mid-1970's, I hitchhiked through central Europe visiting ancient cathedrals and attending the monthly service at the Vatican given by Pope Paul I. Through the years, I would find myself standing near the sacred summit of Uluru (Ayres Rock) in Australia, visiting the monastic ruins on the isle of Skellig Michael and hiking to the top of Croagh Patrick in Ireland, exploring the island of Iona in Scotland, hiking up Bear Butte in South Dakota, trekking to Machu Pichu, listening to the call to prayer in Morocco and dancing in the streets of India during Diwali. Pilgrimage was a logical continuation of this path.

After completing three different pilgrimages, I do not consider myself religious in the traditional sense. What I gleaned from my experiences was a sense of peace and inner calm. Immersing myself in situations where the people around me strived to be their best selves and showed compassion to those around them. The conscious act of pilgrimage forced me into a daily reflection on my faults, sins, loves and relationships. I experienced the therapy of stepping out of my normal life for weeks at a time. It cleared so much noise in my head. I felt the millions of footsteps through time, walking the same paths, visiting the same sacred places and feeling the same calm reflections of spirit.

The Accidental Sadhu

Alaknanda Valley

We had hiked out three hours that morning from Govindghat, India after spending several days visiting the Valley of the Flowers and trekking to the sacred lake, Hemkund. We reached the trailhead at 9:00 AM and were picked up by our driver, Sameer. After a harrowing drive and a traffic jam caused by a landslide that blocked the road, we reached Badrinath, the first temple of the Hindu Char Dham, dedicated to the God Vishnu. We had a quick lunch and then we drove to Mana, the northern-most village in India.

Tim, my long-time friend and trekking partner, had planned

on hiking to a waterfall nearby. Vasundhara Falls at 12,200 feet elevation, was another two miles and a 2,000-foot climb. I was not in the mood for more trekking after our earlier hike and the challenging drive, but I agreed. Tim quickly left me behind and as I trudged forward, my mood became increasingly sour. When I arrived at the waterfall, I dropped my pack and sat in the dirt, exhausted. The view of the Alaknanda Valley was awe-inspiring.

Soon, a voice from up the hill behind me drew my attention from the valley. Sitting above me on some rocks was a shaggy-haired man wrapped in a worn blanket. He motioned for me to join him so I grabbed my bag and scrambled up to his stone shelter. He offered me hot tea that was prepared by his attendant and pointed to the nearby flowers, the tea's main ingredient. As I sat on the stone bench next to him and sipped the peppery herbal tea, I must not have looked out of place with my shoulder length hair and scruffy beard. I marveled at the towering peaks and river valley, the sun turning the water into a snaking sliver of light. I asked the name of one of the peaks and the man laughed as I tried to repeat his words, enjoying my poor pronunciation.

Soon, five men wearing street clothes hiked up the trail and joined us. Taking off their shoes, they knelt down and pressed their heads on the feet of my new friend, a holy man, a sadhu. They then turned and bowed to me; one might say reverence by association. I became an accidental sadhu.

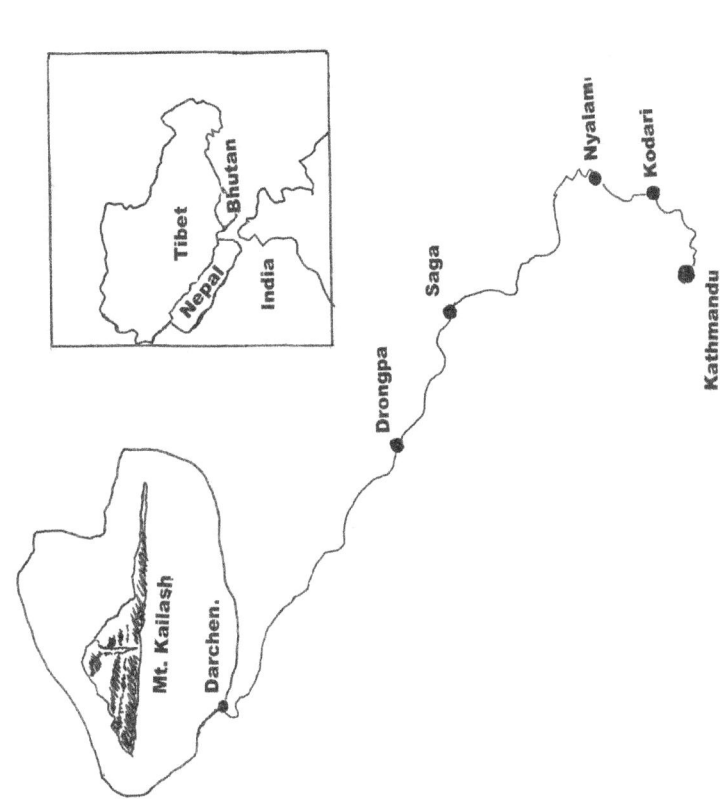

Tibet, A Journey to Mt. Kailash

Mt. Kailash

With the help of my friend and mountain guide, Suzanne Allen, I was able to fulfill my dream to travel to Tibet. Suzanne had guided in Nepal and referred me to a local guide who was able to organize an overland trip from Katmandu into Tibet. I would later lose my dear friend Suzanne who died in a climbing accident while guiding in Alaska.

The kora (circumnavigating) of Mt. Kailash or Kang Rinpoche as it is known to the Tibetans had been a dream of mine for 10 years. Mt. Kailash is sacred to four of the world's religions: Buddhism, Hinduism, Jainism and the Bon. It is also the source of four sacred rivers: Indus, Sutlej, Brahmaputra and the Karnali. Kailash is considered to be the abode of Shiva in Hinduism and the center or navel of the Universe in Buddhism.

Mt. Kailash

The Pilgrimage

I listened to the rain slowly start its pattering, one drop and then another until the night was filled with a steady rhythm broken by occasional thunder in the distance. Half-awake, I dreamt of spring thunderstorms on the Midwestern plains of Nebraska from my childhood. With a cool breeze blowing in through the open window, the sharp smell of the air with the rain's arrival and the low rumble of thunder, I was so calm that I fell into a delicious sleep.

Morning. Light began to fill the room and birds in the courtyard started singing. I climbed out of bed and looked out the window at the wet rooftops. Birds of all shapes and sounds darted between the buildings, while rows of them clung to wires in nervous formation. A damp wetness covered everything. I heard only birds and dripping water. For the third time I was in Kathmandu, Nepal, but this time the journey would lead to Tibet.

With a few days rest to temper the jet lag and make final arrangements, there was an opportunity to revisit some of the places in the city that were becoming familiar. I wandered through the Thamel district to Durbar Square and made the steep climb up the many stone steps of Swayambhunath. One day was spent wandering around the great stupa at Boudhanath. I stood at the entrance of the monastery next to an elderly woman who kneeled and prayed to the statue of Buddha within. Aligned on the floor in the front room were two rows of young monks chanting their lessons. Cymbals rang, horns blew and the sacred texts were sung. A small boy sat elevated on the left row, the reincarnation of the last lama. I stood in the doorway transfixed. Several young men carried buckets of liquefied saffron and poured it on top of the white stucco of the stupa's dome. I bought a small packet and added it to the vat for good luck.

The days passed quickly and with the arrival of our Chinese visas we were finally on our way to Tibet. The trip out of Kathmandu was slow, dusty, and full of honking horns and traffic. The half-built roads became an obstacle course as every car, motorcycle, and bus jockeyed for position. It felt endless and stifling, but eventually the city fell behind and the land became lush and green with farms, villages and brick factories with their tall red kiln smoke stacks. The road climbed higher and wound over lofty hilltops towards the border crossing at Kodari. Past the village of Dalalghat, the road descended steeply to the Indravati River and the end of our drive in Nepal.

Kodari, the main border crossing into the Chinese territory, was a bedlam of vehicles, animals and people. We met our Tibetan liaison who selected a few porters from a frantic crowd of locals to carry our gear across the Freedom Bridge. As we walked across the bridge from Nepal into Tibet, rigid Chinese soldiers in green fatigues stood on each side under a massive billowing red Chinese flag. Entering the heavily armed and unfriendly building, we faced the hard stares of the immigration officials. After handing over my passport to the female soldier, she sternly motioned for me to move to the side. My passport was flagged by the computer with a large red bar at the top of the screen which momentarily had me in a bit of a panic. I was asked if I had "The Book," meaning anything written by or about the Dalai Lama. I said no and after a few minutes, with the help of our liaison officer, I was allowed to pass into Tibet.

Relieved to be out of the immigration building, we met our drivers and support staff who led us through a swarm of currency sellers pressing hard for a sale. Breaking free we jumped into a worn Toyota Land Cruiser and drove at breakneck speed up a winding road to the hillside town of Zhangmu or Dram in Tibetan, at around 7,000 feet in elevation. Zhangmu is a Chinese military garrison offering little beyond hotels, restaurants, neon lit store fronts of prostitutes and more aggressive money changers. We spent one rainy night there before leaving for the Tibetan Plateau. The small, two-bed room had a marvelous view down the river valley and just outside the window several swallows had made mud nests that hung on the vertical wall.

The concrete road ironically called the "Freedom Highway" climbed steeply to our next stop at Nyalam. We left the dense foliage and entered a barren world of high altitude, camping at a grassy spot near a stone house to spend the night at 13,500 feet. Short travel days were needed to acclimatize as we climbed to the 15,000-foot Tibetan Plateau.

That evening we decided to hike up a rise behind our camp. It was a 1,200-foot vertical gain so our hike took us to over 14,500 feet. The wind was blowing hard as we stood on the summit that was covered in prayer flags. Fabric flapped in the wind and carpeted the rocks beneath our feet. Offerings of broken bits of porcelain and clothing lay scattered. I clasped my hands, said a silent prayer, and placed a coin on a rock as my own personal offering. I asked our Tibetan guide the significance of the hill. He said was created by Milarepa, the great Buddhist saint who picked up sand in the palms of his hands and let it fall back to earth like in an hour glass, creating a small hill of dirt. Without knowing it, we had hiked up to a sacred spot, an appropriate first step on our journey to Kailash.

The next morning was filled with sunshine. As we continued our drive, vast snow-covered peaks started breaking the horizon. The ground was brown and rocky. We crested the first of many la (mountain passes). Shishapangma, at over 26,000 feet, loomed large. A gate of prayer flags welcomed us to the Tibetan Plateau, the rooftop of the world, at nearly 16,000 feet in elevation.

A half hour later, we left the main road leading to Lhasa and began the dusty, bone-jarring crawl towards Kailash. Miles and hours battered us as fine sand floated into the cab of the jeep. We tied bandannas around our faces to keep the dust out of our lungs. We passed a cobalt-blue lake whose color bled into a dark purple and brown hill, capped with white clouds. This lake was followed by a second with black waters ringed by ashen alkali. The horizon was dreamlike.

After seven hours of breathing dirt, we arrived at the outskirts of the town of Saga near the blue-green waters of the Brahmaputra River on its journey to India. Our lodging was a small tea house with basic, hard beds and a communal eating area where the owner's small daughter stared and laughed at the foreigners sitting at her table. Sometime during the early evening as I sat drinking tea, attempting to stay warm from the yak dung stove, I dropped into a gentle trance listening to the wind. The whole world was gone for a moment in the wind's calming song.

With the arrival of darkness, loudspeakers blared the nightly Chinese informational proclamations and patriotic music. I slept little with the constant barking of the street dogs that slept during the day and roamed all night.

The following day was another eight hours of bouncing through the desolate countryside over passes that crested near

16,000 feet in elevation. Mid-day we drove through an area of large pastel colored sand dunes with an aqua lake in the distance. Another visual shift from boredom to amazement. The day ended in the village of Pyrang with its mud brick buildings and one street that was littered with trash that took flight with each gust of wind. A dead dog lay on the side of the dirt road. Once more, we had hoped to camp but the water sources were polluted or nonexistent so we procured crude lodging which led to another fitful night's sleep.

The next day's drive was much the same. The Land Cruiser passed Gravel Lake with its swimming pool colored water and gray gravel shore whose soft colors pulled me from a head nodding stupor. Our route traversed two more mountain passes that reached 17,000 feet. The sky remained clear and dark blue.

There was a lengthy delay at a Chinese military checkpoint in the middle of nowhere which seemed designed to harass the Tibetans more than anything else. We had a short panic attack when we initially couldn't find our red stamped visa, but after a desperate round of unpacking, it was found.

We arrived at a rise above Lake Manasarovar, the Lake of Consciousness and Enlightenment, at the end of the day. Mt. Kailash stood clear in the distance and our guide said we had very good karma since the mountain was visible. The landscape was breathtaking. A group of Indian Hindus pulled up, and upon seeing Mt. Kailash, lay on the ground facing the mountain in prayer. I clasped my hands together and pressed them to my head and heart.

Later, I walked to the lake's edge and knelt down, cupping water into my hands. I lifted them and let the drops wet my hair just as I had done two years before at Gaumukh (the headwaters of the Ganges) in India. A large group of Hindus waded into the lake

13

for a ritual bathing. Small waves broke the shore as Kailash floated in the distance.

At sunset, I walked up a sandy hill behind our camp and watched the sun sink behind the lake through a nearly black cloud. A frigid wind hit me as rays of light broke under the cloud reflecting on the lake's graphite waters. The night would bring freezing temperatures. The lakeshore and small inflow streams were frozen by daybreak.

Lake Manasarovar

The Kora

By late morning the following day we had packed our camp and drove the short distance to the town of Darchen for the one-night, government required stay. Darchen was full of debris. Thankfully our night's lodging was a teahouse that sat at the edge of town. After a short meal we decided to take a day hike to Taboche which was about 3 ½ miles away, since we would be driving that first portion of the kora the next day.

The start of our kora led out the front door of the teahouse. The trail worked its way across an open slope and along the shoulders of Kailash. Arriving at Chaktsal Gang Gompa we sat and marveled at the celebratory pole with strings of prayer flags from the recent Saga Dawa Festival. Mt. Kailash's snow-covered crest was brilliant. In the foreground rose a large, flat rock buttress, the sky burial for the local Tibetans. The dead are carried up and dismembered, to be consumed by vultures. The birds are now becoming extinct so packs of wild dogs roam the area, a morbid and frightening thought. I sat looking up at the rampart and felt uneasy. Even my natural curiosity could not get me to visit its heights.

The next morning was freezing. We left Darchen and drove to Taboche. The light was just starting to strike the top of the ridge as we began our hike up a narrow gorge with sandstone-colored cliffs that loomed over us. New snow clung to the orange, rocky spires above. We made good time as the path was fairly flat, each setting our own rhythm. Our guide walked behind me, rolling his strand of prayer beads in his hand and chanting softly as we kept to the right side of a rocky stream bed. Near a large carved rock were piles of

15

stacked stones. Each of us added our own small stone.

Nearing midday, a Tibetan couple rode by on a motorcycle. They hadn't gotten too far in front of us when the bike came to a sputtering stop. Approaching, we saw them struggling to push it up a steep section of the trail. My friend and I smiled and offered to help and the four of us pushed it to the top of the rise, our first good deed.

I soon pulled ahead of the group and relished hiking in my own company. As the trail rolled over another rocky bulge of earth, I looked ahead at a pilgrim stretched out on the dirt. His arms reached out in front of his body where he would mark the ground, stand and walk to his mark, where he would lay down once again. He was demonstrating his devotion to his faith, something fewer and fewer are now choosing to do. As I stepped to the left to pass, the pilgrim looked up at me and motioned for water. I dropped my pack and pulled out my water bottle. As he stood up and opened his mouth, I unscrewed the lid and gave him a drink. He swallowed and nodded for more, and once again I filled his mouth with water. Finished, he looked into my eyes, bowed his head and returned to his prostrations. I gathered my pack and as I walked away it began to lightly snow even though the sun was still shining. The clouds parted and Mt. Kailash appeared. Snowflakes mixed with tears as I walked on in solitude.

Our camp for the night was below the north face of the mountain. Avalanches powdered off the upper reaches and the sun's setting rays touched the summit ridges. Hanging glaciers became illuminated with the movement of light. As the sun set on Kailash, I felt the deep significance of being here, at this place in this moment. It felt like I had been drawn here for an eternity of lives.

The next day was grueling as we pushed on for 10 hours to Dolma-la Pass at 18,600 feet elevation. We caught up with a mass of pilgrims, a procession of horses with their elderly riders and those walking slowly, struggling up the pass. We stopped at Shiva-tsal, a place of death and renewal. Buddhists believe that by leaving a personal item at this sacred place, pilgrims undergo a symbolic death, acknowledging their impermanence and leaving their old life behind. By leaving this offering it is said to purge all bad karma. I left a small stocking cap on the pile of clothing.

We continued through the high altitude at a slow pace and arrived at the summit that was covered in prayer flags. I took a silk scarf that I had carried from Kathmandu and tied it to a string

Mani Stones

17

of flags. One of our support staff tied a new strand of colored prayer flags to the pile. It moved with the breeze as if it was a beast bound to the snow and ice. I spent an hour sitting in the sun and gazing at the surroundings before walking the rocky trail down the other side of the pass above the sacred lake, Gauri Kund, the Lake of Compassion. I caught up with the others of our group at an extraordinary pile of Mani stones with their intricate devotional carvings. It would be hours before we would finally reach our next camp near a small stream. Exhausted, I slept a sleep filled with vivid dreams.

The morning brought snow. I laid in my warm sleeping bag and listened to the snow pelting the tent's fabric. A horse snorted and neighed nearby. The wind picked up and once dressed, I stood outside in the swirling air. Our group's yaks squatted on the ground dusted white with the flakes. I turned into the wind and felt it on my face, enjoying the harshness of the mountains.

We packed and headed back out on the main trail through the snow. We passed a small village where livestock were pressed up against the houses to avoid the wind. After another hour, we began to see the edge of the clouds and walked into sunshine. We turned to look back at a wall of black clouds. The hills were now dusted white and Kailash again rose above us below a cerulean sky as we hiked along a narrow but spectacular gorge. Soon we were in Darchen and back at the beginning of the kora. We shook hands and hugged one another. It was complete.

We climbed into our Land Cruiser for a short drive to Lake Manasarovar and a camp near the 8th century Chui Gompa Monastery. After we pitched our tents near the shore, I hiked up a hill with prayer flags and sat alone watching the wind push shadows across the water. Kailash appeared and once again

18

confirmed our good karma. We had seen the mountain every day since arriving.

We spent a couple days camped at the lake and took advantage of the time by hiking to the monastery that sits perched on top of a pyramid of rock. Astonishing views rewarded us. As I stood awestruck by the azure waters, I mulled over the idea of past lives and why I, in this life, am drawn to wandering, searching for something in myself. I have traveled to places where I have suffered physically, left loved ones who mean everything to me behind, and come close to dying. I still always go.

The return trip to Kathmandu retraced the arduous 507 miles over the windswept Tibetan Plateau. There were the same dusty camps and mud brick lodgings in Pyrang. We had the opportunity to watch a Japanese martial arts movie translated into Tibetan and were entertained by two young children having an argument, each armed with a sharpened stick and rake. No blood drawn, but nearly as entertaining as the movie.

The evening in Saga was spent sitting in front of a small yak dung stove drinking beer from small shot glasses that our host kept filling. My friend Frank and I sat in front of the glow of the stove and discussed how we live and waste so much with our Western lifestyles.

The next day, our Land Cruiser outpaced the truck and we stopped near a small stream to wait. Our driver laid on the ground to take advantage of the time out of the car. Two young Tibetan women who looked to be in their late teens or early twenties walked up to where we were sitting and tried to make conversation. They were both quite striking, with beautiful smiles.

A Mercedes sedan came up the road and got stuck in the middle of the stream due to the number of rocks in the path.

19

Official looking Chinese men sat in the back while the driver got out and stood in the water, pushing rocks aside. He called out to the two women to help. They stood in the water and lifted the stones to the side while the men sat in the back of the Mercedes. I looked down at our driver who opened one eye and smiled, acting as if he was asleep. Once the sedan was on its way, the women walked back over to the Land Cruiser and silently sat waiting for our truck to arrive. The new road being built uses Tibetan manual labor and these two women were part of a work crew who lived in tents near the stream.

When our truck arrived, our cook made a huge lunch. The two women were invited to join us but they refused. After we were finished, our cook wrapped up what remained and gave it to them. They were very thankful for the provisions. It was a rare treat in their hard lives.

Our last night in Tibet was in Zhangmu. It rained hard all evening and we ventured out, passing the neon lit windows with their sad looking hostesses that reflected a strange beauty on the stone streets. Drenched, we changed into some dry but not clean clothes and joined our crew for a final dinner where we ate, laughed, and voiced our sincere appreciation for their work. We had become friends.

The morning was rushed as we loaded up the trucks to drive to the valley floor and the Freedom Bridge where we would once again cross into Nepal. Unfortunately, just outside of town at the first tight curve, a large truck had overturned, blocking the whole road. Lines of local Tibetans shouldered boxes of apples from the spilled bed and shuttled the produce up and around the truck's carcass. A small gap around one end of the truck allowed just enough room for the narrow Chinese mini vans to squeeze through. Our Tibetan guide hailed one of the minivan drivers and paid him to drive us down the road to the border crossing.

We quickly said our goodbyes to our Tibetan friends and I sadly realized that I would never see them again. I felt I had accomplished something I began dreaming of over ten years ago. My new friends told me that it took ten years for my karma to be right for this trip. I believe they spoke the truth.

Chiu Gompa

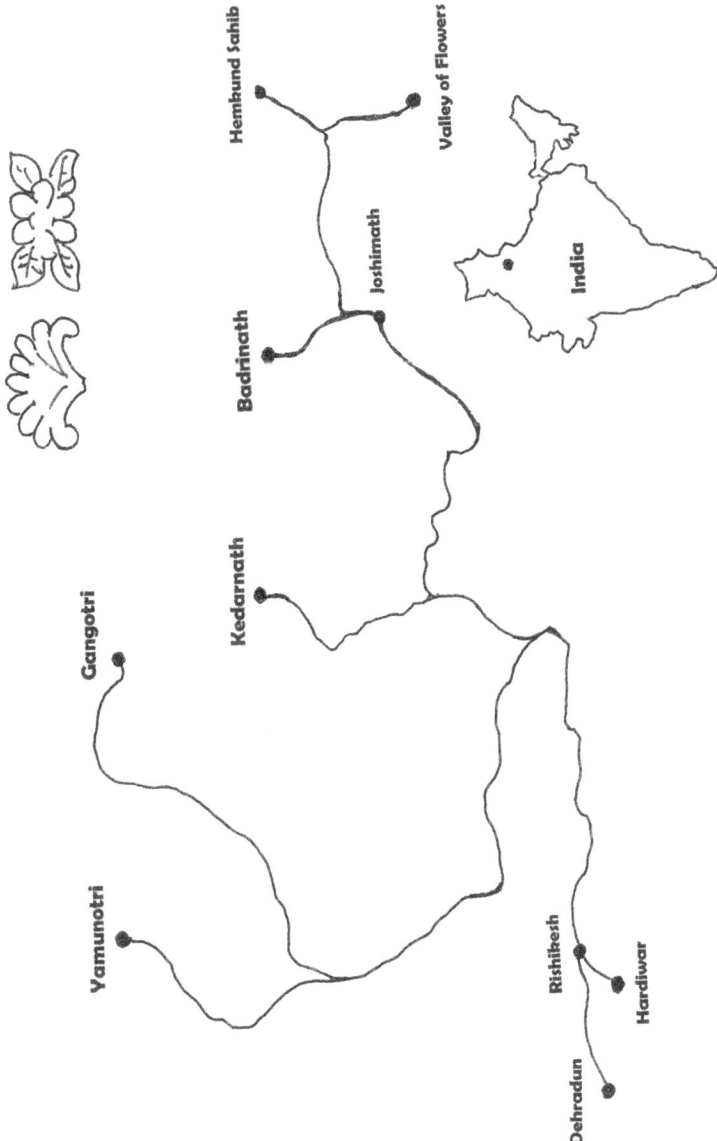

Hemkund Sahib

Valley of Flowers

Joshimath

India

Badrinath

Gangotri

Kedarnath

Yamunotri

Rishikesh

Hardiwar

Dehradun

India and the Four Abodes, Travels on the Char Dham

As I arrived in India, the assault on my senses was complete. Noise and odors hit you hard in New Delhi. I exited the gate after nearly 18 hours of air travel and a missed connecting flight. The weight of the duffle pulled against my shoulders as I pushed myself into the crowd of bodies. Sameer, Tim's friend and our driver, held a small white card as he pressed against a railing. His presence eased my fears and helped us avoid the throng of aggressive taxi drivers trying to recruit passengers. Sameer greeted us as Tim Sir and Kim Sir, how he would refer to us throughout the trip.

Outside a light rain hit my face as I looked up into the sky. The monsoons had not yet finished in northern India, so at least the air was better than I expected. The drive to Dehra Dun over the next few hours was through an onslaught of honking horns and thick clouds of exhaust. Outside the windows of our small diesel car was mayhem; people, cows, tut tuts, cars, trucks, buses and tractors, all aggressively vying for a spot on the narrow road. We were just beyond the airport when a car and bus accident blocked the road. After such a long plane ride I was dazed but soon stopped flinching at the near collisions and the sudden red glow of brake lights as I began to trust Sameer's driving ability.

As we pulled away from the central part of New Delhi I looked across to a mountain of garbage with hundreds of huge circling black birds. It felt to me like a story book omen. We drove on dodging oncoming buses and crushing traffic that never quite moved over far enough, but somehow, we always squeezed by. Eventually Sameer left the main highway. We found ourselves

Ganges

driving on a one lane road with red brick shoulders along the muddy brown Ganga canal through farmlands of sugar cane, corn and rice fields. Other than a random oncoming car, the common mode of transportation here seemed to be either tractor or bicycle. We passed through terrain of green damp vegetation with muted gray skies, occasionally filled with brilliant white egrets. Several large hawks flew alongside, searching for road kill. Groups of monkeys sat with mothers clutching small babies. Large water buffalo pushed one another aside for the best grazing spot or toiled by pulling carts overflowing with recently cut reeds. A woman in a brilliant orange sari walked barefoot on a mud path. A sleeping dog lay in the middle of the road that Sameer dubbed "The King of the Road." I draped my arms out the car's window and inhaled; eucalyptus trees, rain, vegetation, cooking food, exhaust, burning trash, and incense. This was India and I was filled with awe.

It was Friday at 1:00 PM and Sameer needed to stop to pray at a small mosque. We stayed behind and waited for an hour as rain pelted the car. We were in the company of a Muslim taking us on a Hindu pilgrimage, only in India where any path to God seems to work.

It took us nearly seven hours of driving to reach Dehra Dun where we checked into a small hotel and headed straight to the bar for a few Haywards 5000 Super Strong Beer to numb our bodies and brains after all the hours of travel. A group of high school boys sat at a table near us. They all had just failed their engineering exams which were critical for future education and job prospects and were working on cheering themselves up with Haywards in very large bottles Seeing us nearby they picked up their school books and joined our table. Because of my long hair, they thought I was pretty "cool" and wanted to find out who I was. I found this

27

humorous and enjoyed talking with them and telling stories behind a growing number of empty bottles. Eventually, we headed to bed.

After several hours of deep sleep, I looked at my watch and thought we had overslept and were late meeting Sameer. I sat up and yelled across the room to Tim that we were late and we needed to get moving. He looked at his watch and told me to shut up and go back to sleep. It was only 11:00 PM the same evening and we had only been asleep for a few hours. Something happens to you after days of traveling, a twelve and a half hour time difference and too many beers on the opposite side of the planet.

Rishikish

It took an hour and a half to drive the 30-mile, rain-filled road to Rishikish, the yoga center of the world. We found a pleasant hotel and after dropping our luggage set out to explore the town. Our first excursion was across a narrow suspension bridge that airily hung over the brown waters of the Ganges. We shuffled past pedestrian traffic and dodged occasional motorcycles that took up most of the bridge's walking space. Getting too close to the pylons, we had to move to the side to avoid the reach of monkeys that clawed and snarled as we walked past. One grabbed Tim's shirt with a tight grip causing a tug of war. On the opposite bank was the orange, coned-shaped roof of Tera Manzil, a Hindu temple. Its 13 floors of small shrines pay homage to a host of Gods and Goddesses. The deities are said to fulfill prayers. "Couldn't hurt," I thought to myself as I silently prayed and rang the numerous large bells. I made my way to a small nook looking down to the Ganges. I watched three women in red saris and a man in a turquoise shirt bend down and scoop water into their hands as they stood on the large steps, the sacred water lapping over their feet. It was hard to leave such a beautiful place.

We wandered the shops in hope of finding a lunch spot. There was a cafe being advertised by a huge man painted white and only draped in a linen cloth, portraying a Hindu god. The whole scene was surreal. Wandering Rishikish you become aware of the number of Westerners strolling the streets. Gurus and Sadhus line the sidewalks with Western disciples in tow. It seemed to me that many of the foreigners looked like they were just trying too hard to find that "something." I know now that looking doesn't always result in finding what you need.

Shiva

After lunch we sat on stone steps that entered the Ganges. The air was humid and between the sweat and short rain bursts I never really felt dry. A large white sculpture of Shiva sat cross-legged in a pose of meditation on a slab of concrete that hovered just above the rushing water. Sitting on the steps, a small pup came up to me wagging its tail, looking at me with sweet eyes. The number of stray dogs that roam the streets in India is heartbreaking. I let it sit next to me, knowing its short life would be a struggle, but at least for a moment it wasn't alone. Being in a safe place, it pressed hard against me. I was sad to leave it, but it was time to move on.

Valley of the Flowers

The following day we drove 10 hours to the town of Joshimath. The day's adventure began within the first ten minutes of leaving Rishikish where we had to jump out of the car and move several large rocks that blocked the road. Shortly afterward we crossed a metal one-lane bridge that had me wondering if it would hold our weight. Sameer referred to the creaking as "music." I had a strong sense of déjà vu that unnerved me as we crossed.

Past the bridge were a series of shacks whose walls were made of flattened diesel barrels with black plastic tarp roofs, a sign of the difficult life of the manual laborers. I flinched repeatedly as we came inches from hitting oncoming trucks, blaring their horns. We had many near misses. The route north was in ruin. Rock slides, piles of rubble, and large stones lay in the middle of the road forcing us to weave around them and at times come dizzyingly close to an edge that dropped straight down into the rushing Ganges. Humorous signs were posted as warnings: "Speed thrills, but often kills"; "Eager to last, then why so fast?"; "After whiskey, driving is risky."

We arrived at our destination in exactly 10 hours, just as Sameer had estimated. Joshimath sits below two mountains, one shaped like a reclining elephant and the other a sleeping woman. The small disheveled town had a basic tourist hotel that was inexpensive and had electricity that didn't come on until 10:00 PM at night. That's just the way things are in India.

The next morning Sameer arrived at 6:30 AM for the 13-mile drive to Govindghat. As we climbed up the other side of the valley the scenery was spectacular. By noon, we arrived at Govindghat and started the eight-mile walk to the village of Ghangaria. Sameer

31

walked us to the trailhead after purchasing three bright orange head scarves to cover our hair, and then led us into a Sikh temple for a blessing for a safe trek. Exiting the temple, there was orange all around us. A large rock painted orange, dried orange leaves on the ground, the temple walls and scarves that covered all our heads all seemed to shout out the bold color.

It was a 4,000-foot climb to Ghangaria. We found a small lodge that provided shelter from the steady rain that pelted the metal roof throughout the night. I slept well until the hotel's generator kicked on at 5:00 AM, shaking the whole room and filling it with exhaust fumes. Because of it, we were on the trail as the sun rose. We were able to work our way through the horse trains of pilgrims who were heading to Hemkund, and with a lot of maneuvering, mostly avoided the ankle-deep muck of mud and horse droppings.

We reached the trail divide for the Valley of the Flowers and quickly entered a pine tree forest that lined a beautiful raging river. After climbing steeply, we eventually entered the opening of the valley. It was spectacular with towering snow-covered peaks on both sides and numerous waterfalls slicing their way through the rock. We crossed a poorly constructed bridge made of boards and sheet metal to a viewpoint at a large rock that provided a panorama. It was here that Tim had left some of his father's ashes the year before. I looked up at the sky. The sun was highlighting the rim of a large cloud. I remembered his father and his wonderful sense of humor. At that moment, I had a sensation that he was happy that I was standing next to his son, a good friend.

After hiking to the end of the valley, I turned around to look at the full length of the Valley of the Flowers. The smell of damp vegetation filled my lungs. About halfway back, I found a flat rock near a stream crossing where I laid down and felt the intense heat of the sun as it broke through the clouds. Beautiful orange butterflies hovered nearby and one settled on my knee. I meditated with my eyes shut and pictured the scenery, vivid and clear. As I slowed my breath, I promised myself to live the most honorable life possible. When I opened my eyes, I noticed a black bird perched on a rock patiently watching me with a rolling eye. At that moment I realized I was truly on a personal pilgrimage.

Hemkund Sahib

We made it back to the hotel just as it began to rain, with water cascading from the roof. Tim leaned over to me and said, "somebody's God is smiling on us today." The belching generator woke us again the next morning, way too early. We ate a simple breakfast with black tea and left the guest house around 6:00 AM. There were no rain clouds for the day's climb to the sacred Sikh pilgrimage site of Hemkund Sahib, 15,197 feet in elevation. The sun illuminated the glacial peaks at the head of the valley with an amazing pink alpenglow. We managed to get in front of a throng of pilgrims and the horses that would carry many of the less physically able Sikhs.

The path to Hemkund climbed relentlessly and I plodded along, gradually passing the procession of smiling faces, words of encouragement, and offers of candy. The view across the valley was stunning and reinforced the beauty of the day. There were a series of temporary shacks called dhabas a few hours up the trail that sold food and drink and we stopped for a cup of black tea which invigorated me for the final long push to the top. The trail transitioned from mud to snow and ice as I approached 15,000 feet in elevation. I began to walk with a young Sikh man. We chatted about a litany of subjects and as we neared the end he asked if I was going to bathe in the lake and if so, I should do so as soon as I arrived. With my body temperature raised due to the climbing, the icy submersion would be more tolerable. If I stood around too long, I would get too cold to face the chilly waters of Hemkund. I didn't reflect much before making my decision.

I arrived at the crest and before me stood a Sikh temple and the lake. Seven peaks wrapped around the blue water, each

Hemkund

one with a flag on its summit. There was a large shelter full of
pilgrims removing their clothing. The men stripped down to their
underwear and unwrapped their turbans, letting their long hair
drop below their shoulders. I watched as they stepped into the
water, sat and immersed themselves six times in the ice-cold lake.
Ancient looking men sat in meditation somehow ignoring the cold
water. The lake devoted to Guru Gobind Singh seemed to draw
me towards the water. Without thinking I removed my clothes
and walked barefoot over a thin layer of snow to the lake's edge
and down the submerged steps. I don't think I took a breath as I
dunked six times, rose and exited the water. Several Sikhs gave me
huge smiles and bows as this white-bodied, long-haired foreigner
sought his clothes.

I quickly got dressed and stood against a sun-warmed wall of the temple to get some heat back into my core. Feeling slightly warmer, I walked around the corner and an elderly Sikh walked up to me with a cheerful face. He shook my hand and proceeded to tell me that I was a very lucky man. He then directed me to the temple where a rotund man sat on the floor and served me from a massive metal bowl of steaming rice. I ate rice and drank chai and when I was about to leave another group of pilgrims insisted that I come back with them for more. I finally slipped away thinking that the multiple meals would surely be the test of my stomach's fortitude. The sun was blindingly bright as I descended into the valley. Below, large eagles soared back and forth as thin clouds of mist rose skyward. As I stopped and watched the birds, I squinted in the brightness at the landscape and thought yes, I am a very lucky man.

Badrinath

The next day started like the previous two with the belching diesel generator. After a quick bite we walked the eight miles downhill to Govind Ghat and Sameer. It was another exceptionally beautiful morning full of good wishes from happy Sikh pilgrims heading towards Hemkund. Sameer stood leaning against his car even though we were two hours earlier than we had agreed. Our early departure was for naught because a half hour down the road we were stopped by a massive backup of vehicles. The road had been damaged by a large landslide from the previous two days of rain. The road had just reopened but was a sloppy and muddy lane that only allowed one vehicle to proceed at a time. Our timing must have been good because it was the downhill traffic's turn to traverse the slide area. Workers stood every 500 feet with hand held radios and small flags watching the hillside and waving frantically and blowing whistles to get each car across the sections as fast as possible. It was truly frightening as we drove down the slick track with a mountain stream on one side, and a steep dirt slope with house-sized boulders barely resting in place, on the other. Sameer just looked up and said it was in God's hands.

After several hours of driving, we finally arrived at Badrinath, the first temple of the Hindu Char Dham, dedicated to the go Vishnu. We had a quick lunch and then drove to Mana, the northern-most village in India. Tim had planned on hiking to a waterfall nearby. Vasundhara Falls at 12,200 feet elevation, was another two miles and a 2,000-foot climb. I was not in the mood for more trekking after our earlier hike and the challenging drive, but I agreed. Tim quickly left me behind and as I trudged forward, my mood became increasingly sour. When I arrived at the waterfall,

Badrinath

I dropped my pack and sat in the dirt, exhausted. The view of the Alaknanda Valley was awe-inspiring.

Soon, a voice from up the hill behind me drew my attention from the valley. Sitting above me on some rocks was a shaggy-haired man wrapped in a worn blanket. He motioned for me to join him so I grabbed my bag and scrambled up to his stone shelter. He offered me hot tea that was prepared by his attendant and pointed to the nearby flowers, the tea's main ingredient. As I sat on the stone bench next to him and sipped the peppery herbal tea, I must not have looked out of place with my shoulder length hair and scruffy beard. I marveled at the towering peaks and river valley, the sun turning the water into a snaking sliver of light. I asked the name of one of the peaks and the man laughed as I tried to repeat his words, enjoying my poor pronunciation.

Soon, five men wearing street clothes hiked up the trail and joined us. Taking off their shoes, they knelt down and pressed their heads on the feet of my new friend, a holy man, a sadhu. They then turned and bowed to me; one might say reverence by association. I became an accidental sadhu.

Even though the day's light was fading fast, Sameer insisted that we drive a few miles past the village of Mana to what he referred to as the last tea house in India. After a quick tea, we drove back to Badrinath and I hobbled as quickly as I could across a bridge to the base of the temple, dedicated to the God Vishnu. I shot a few frames with my camera of the ornately carved outer walls and the line of pilgrims waiting to enter. The town was swarming with pilgrims and there seemed to be beggars everywhere. They were difficult to ignore.

The next morning was frigid and our diesel car would not start until it warmed up. While we waited, two young Hindus walked up and said hello. They had noticed that I was staring at the beautiful morning light illuminating the mountains that towered into the sky above us. One of them looked up at the peaks and said that the two mountains we were looking at were sacred and that God lived there, that God prayed for all mankind no matter what their religion.

Kedarnath

We drove back to Joshimath and stayed two nights before an eight-hour drive to the next temple on our quest, Kedarnath. Just outside Joshimath was a cable car to the off-season ski area, Auli. The sunshine and views of Nanda Devi and surrounding mountain range were brilliant, and I sat and sketched a few drawings while Tim went for a hike. We caught the afternoon cable car back to town where we asked Sameer if there was any chance of finding a beer. He asked around and drove us to a shoulder-wide alley with steep steps. Halfway down was a door with a small window with a man standing behind it selling bottles of Haywards 5000. We stood in line with the local men patiently waiting their turn. We quickly put the beer in our backpacks as it is officially illegal to have alcohol in the district. After finishing our first beers, we went back to purchase a second round. Sameer stopped by our room later to watch our television. His favorite show was on that evening - an Indian version of American Bandstand. During the tv show he was insistent we learn some dance steps. It was quite entertaining and we were thankful no one else saw us.

Ah, the dogs of India. They sleep all day and prowl, bark, and fight all night, resulting in no sleep for us humans. After a night of barking dogs and with a bit of a hangover, we were on our way to Kedarnath. The winding rural road climbed into the hill country, past cliff edge villages and terraced rice fields. Sunshine gave everything a radiant glow and the forest of pine trees shimmered. Occasionally, our path was blocked by a water buffalo who would stand firmly in the middle of the road until it felt the desire to move. Families of monkeys watched us with hopeful eyes for any leftover food that might be flung from the car window. At one point

Kedarnath

a line of marigold flowers formed a yellow procession of color.

We drove from Charnoli to Chopta on a one-lane paved road through a musk deer sanctuary. Unfortunately, we did not see any of the elusive animals. I hung out the window breathing the warm clear air of the jungle with climbing vines snaking their way up the tree trunks and the constant sound of cicadas. The day was one of the most relaxing and uninhabited sections so far. Not having to endure honking horns, traffic and the crush of humanity was such a relief.

By mid-day we stopped at Chopta and hiked four miles up to the 1,000-year-old temple of Tungnath, revered by Lord Shiva devotees. It's one of the highest Shiva temples in the world. The views were idyllic but I was tired and hot by the time we returned to the car. We continued our journey and arrived at a hotel in Rampur, not far from the trail to the second temple of the Char Dham, Kedarnath. The hotel sat on a bluff above a river in a quiet spot that provided a much-needed good night's sleep.

The next morning, I had a difficult time waking up. The quiet of Rampur was divine; no generators kicking on before sunrise, no barking dogs, yelling people or honking cars, just the pleasant sound of the river. We drove a few miles to the trailhead at Gaurikund and hiked eight miles and over 5,000 vertical feet to Kedranath. The sun was glorious but there was little warmth. My pace was painfully slow as the trail quickly gained elevation. At a half-way point, there was a portable shack selling drinks and snacks where I purchased a lukewarm Fanta orange soda that provided the boost of energy that fueled me to Kedranath, where Tim was patiently waiting once again. We were able to secure a room in another hotel that was basic and cold for an outrageous 800 rupees.

It was still early in the day so we decided to visit the temple of Kedranath. The shrine was built in the 8th century by Adi Sankaracharya to honor Shiva. The large protruding stone that the temple is built over is believed to be the hump of Shiva's shoulder when he disguised himself as a bull and dove into the earth to avoid the Pandavas. I removed my shoes and slowly walked around the outer walls of the main sanctuary, avoiding the waving hands of begging sadhus. A rotund priest approached us and invited us to join in a puja (prayer). He dabbed a red ink spot known as a tikka in the middle of our foreheads and led us through the entry into a jammed room of chanting voices and clanking bells. Shoulder to shoulder we inched our way through the throng of worshipers to the large rock that protruded from the stone floor, the remnant of Shiva's hump. Circling the rock, we each took turns pouring liquid on the stone. The priest had us press our foreheads to the wet rock and dabbed dampened rice onto our foreheads. We exited into the cold air, confused and dazed, trying to grasp what had just occurred. The whole event was dreamlike and beyond any previous experience. I headed straight back to the hotel and crawled into my sleeping bag, exhausted.

The next morning, we were awakened by a scurrying rat running under our beds that ended any notion of staying in our warm sleeping bags. We decided to brave the chill and walk up to a small shrine about a half hour above our lodging for sunrise. The morning light reached the tops of the peaks above Kedranath making the cold of the early morning worth the effort. As the town became bathed in the morning light, we decided to head back and gather our belongings to start the hike down the valley to meet Sameer.

Sameer picked us up and informed us that we would be taking a detour to another temple, Trijugi Narayan. I thought to myself, "please not another bloody temple." This one was situated at the top of a long, terraced hill. A number of excited children immediately surrounded the car and led us to the sacred spot where the Shiva had married Parvati. Married couples make the pilgrimage for a blessing and a small handful of ash from the fire that has burned for centuries. By visiting and taking the ash home, one is guaranteed a long and successful marriage. We entered the front door of the central chamber where a smoldering fire filled the room with smoke. The priest placed his ash covered thumb to my forehead and asked me to help put a log on the eternal fire, then shook my hand and said that he would see me in the next life and the next and the next. I thanked him and thought what a long way

I have to go if indeed I will return so many more times before I get it right.

Back on the road, we had another five hours of driving to Rudraprayag. We were 11 days into the trip and I was weary. It felt like I had been in this country a very long time. The intensity of India is a constant sensory overload and time moves slowly. We arrived in Rudraprayag and found a small private hotel that was basic and ok by Indian standards and even came with a very large gecko who hung upside down on the ceiling. The air was extremely humid and we spent the evening sweating and sitting on a veranda drinking beer. Dogs were barking all around us so the expectation of sleep didn't look too promising. Rudraprayag was the home of the man-eating leopard who at the turn of the century killed 125 people until it was finally shot by the well know hunter Jim Corbett. Of course, my dreams that night were of running from floor to floor while being chased by a very large cat.

The next morning, I awoke and sat on the veranda, sipping hot black tea and watching the sunlight work its way across the grass. A young woman in a green and gold sari stood on a flat roof across the grounds, gleaning rice in a large wicker bowl. A fine dust rose into the golden light of the morning sun. Tossing the contents upward with a rhythmic twist she caught the falling kernels while lifting the husks skyward. I sat on the deck listening to the cicadas and the dry rustling song of a harvest being gleaned. It was a moment of exceptional beauty.

Rishikesh

We had several hours in the car to reach Rishikesh where we would spend three days of rest. Sameer had requested a break in our schedule to spend time with his girlfriend on the anniversary of their first date. Sameer is Muslim and his girlfriend is Hindu so even though they are quite in love they both know that their families will never allow them to wed. He carried much pain in his heart. On the drive we passed a funeral procession. Several men carried a corpse draped in white fabric. A wreath of orange flowers hung over the sides of the deceased. I watched until the group disappeared behind some trees. During dinner that night, the sun set and I thought of the funeral procession and the soul that had left that life. The orange sun dropped below the horizon into the Indian haze and I sat silently. The sun drifted downwards in the softest light I had ever experienced and my thoughts went back to the draping orange wreath and the white-shrouded body. India is love, wonder, pain and death all on display.

Hardiwar

The following day, we climbed into our car for a day trip and another terrifying drive, this time to Hardiwar. We had the whole day for the visit as we were planning on observing the Aariti ceremony that evening. After our arrival we took a tram to a temple, Chanda Devi, that sits on the top of a high hill. It was cooler at the higher altitude and a nice reprieve from the heat.

A row of women and small children sat on the steps, each with outstretched hands begging for change. Sameer placed a coin in each of their hands and told us that it is important in his faith to make a gesture to the less fortunate. The women were all widows and begging was one of the few options they had for income. Beggars, either without arms or legs, small children and the destitute line many of the streets. There are camps along the river with whole communities living under black plastic tarps and you realize that the children running between the shelters will most likely live this same life as an adult. The poverty is overwhelming. Once at the temple, I sat on a stone bench high above the river valley. I watched a large thin cloud spread out in the sky as if it was being smeared by a knife held in God's hand.

Just before sunset we found a place to sit at the Har Ki Pairi Ghat and the steps that lined the Ganges River. Large numbers of worshipers began to line the banks in a festive mood full of laughter and voice. Several children swam and pulled stringed magnets with the hope of securing coins that had been thrown in the water as an offering. Other people prayed while standing in waist deep water as the holy river slowly lapped over the stone steps where we sat. Vendors sold small, reed boats as offerings, containing flowers and candles. As darkness fell there was a ringing of bells and gongs, torches were lit and directly across the river the priests began to sing. The crowd began to chant along with the priests and those that had purchased the leaf vessels let them float, each carrying a personal prayer. Torches illuminated the far shore and the dark water glimmered with floating candles sparkling in the current. I was amazed, humbled and joyous to be part of this spiritual event. Once the ceremony ended, I shook hands with a man who sat next to me. He wished God's watch over me on my journey.

Gangotri

After another day's rest in Rishikesh we were back on the road for a 12-hour drive to Gangotri, our third temple of the Char Dham. After six hours, we stopped at the village Uttarkashi to get our trekking permits for Tapovan and to replenish the car's empty fuel tank. The permit process went smoothly but the only gas station in the area was out of fuel. We waited in line with what seemed to be every car in the town for two hours in searing heat for the fuel truck to arrive. Luckily, we were towards the front of the line and filled up before the station's supply was depleted once again.

Shortly after leaving Utterkashi the pavement ended at a massive hydroelectric project that reduced our road to rocks, mud, and running streams of water with sections of significant landslide danger. Once again, we held on and trusted both Sameer's driving and God. Our route eventually improved and the road soon hugged a narrow, deep canyon with towering pine trees and an emerald river that tumbled below. Wild sage formed pink swatches of color under the pines that had their limbs trimmed up to 10 feet for firewood. With the grazing of the local animals and the need for home heating, the area appeared to be a finely manicured city park. It just was too tidy for nature. Night fell and for the remaining hour to Gangotri we moved cautiously on the one lane road. After 12 hours of driving the only lodging was a tiny room with a small cafe that provided food that was as bad as the sleeping arrangements.

We didn't get much sleep since our room was under the hotel's kitchen and it felt like the cooking and cleaning went on until dawn. After morning tea we took a short walk to the Gangotri temple where we left our shoes and visited the sanctuary. When we exited, we ended up having to pose with two separate groups

Chanda Devi

Gangotri

of Indian pilgrims who wanted their picture taken with two foreign white boys. I was not sure what that was all about. We eventually started our trek to Tapovan and Gaumukh. The trail was easy to find and the weather was perfect. We arrived at the entrance gate to the national park where we were charged an additional fee for our permit plus an extra charge per camera. It seemed like bribery to me but I was the one visiting their country.

The first five miles followed a river beneath the peaks of the Bhagirathi and were quite stunning. We hadn't quite reached the village of Chirbasa when I passed a person coming down the trail. For some reason I jumped up on the stone barrier on the river side of the path as we passed each other, tripping and barely catching myself. A fall to the river would have been fatal. I stopped once back on the trail and shook my head at such a dumb move.

Someone was watching over me once again, saving me from myself.

It was a scorching hot day and when we came upon a waterfall that layered the slab rock in a thin glaze, I pressed my hands against the wet stone and let the water flow over them. Next came the side of my face and the cold water ran down my neck and pushed up against my hair. The wet stone breathed life and coolness into me.

At Chirbasa, the small tea shops were closed for the season so we found some shade under a small grove of silver barked birch trees with leaves of bright yellow. A herd of Ibex sheep had taken up residence among the boulders and stood above us with steadfast stares. We had to trek another three miles to Bhojbasa in the heat before arriving at the tourist lodge which we nicknamed the "Shitty Hotel." The building had been partially destroyed by an avalanche and the few intact rooms were all occupied. Our only option was to sleep in a large canvas tent with eight wood-framed beds. We were once again sleeping near a power generator which sputtered all night. That mixed with snoring and the smell of another lodger who had a applied a liberal dose of Ben Gay, made it a night of endurance.

By dawn, we were hiking on a well-marked trail that led up a valley along the left side of the Bhagirathi River and entered the jumbled rock and ice of a lateral glacial moraine. We soon arrived at the base of the glacier and watched as silted water raged beneath the ice. This was Gaumukh, The Mouth of the Cow, and the birthplace of the Ganges River. I stood momentarily and stared down at the sacred Hindu site. The two of us hiked through some exceedingly rough terrain for several miles all the time looking for the flat meadow of Tapovan. Nothing looked like a haven in all the jumbled ice and rock. Finally, we stood above a massive ice canyon and realized we were lost. We turned around and began retracing

51

our path when several porters carrying huge loads of climbing gear appeared from one of the large gorges that intersected the glacier. We asked one of the porters where Tapovan was located and he pointed across the wide glacier to the other side. We had made a huge error.

After hiking miles back to Gaumukh, I sat down on a large rock, tired and angry. We could see a faint trail in the dirt that dropped down onto the glacier and after some convincing I got up and stumbled across to the distant rise. Hand over hand we climbed up a steep loose dirt and boulder strewn cliff to the brown flat meadow of Tapovan at over 14,000 feet elevation. Tim and I were greeted by a long-haired skeleton of a Sadhu. He waved in our direction and we joined him for a hot cup of tea that was brewed on a reflector that looked like a satellite dish that used the sun's rays to heat water. We toured his cave, a slot in the stone wall about four feet high, where he had lived for the last 15 years in solitude and meditation. Woolen rugs and blankets covered the cave's floor. Living for so long in the claustrophobic hole did not seem inviting. We declined his offer of rice but donated 100 rupees each as an offering, as a way to exit his overzealous invitation for further conversation.

We walked across the meadow to a spot next to a small stream. I spent time gathering stones to build a wind break to shelter my frail looking bivy sack, all the time staring up at the sheer walls of Mt. Shivling, the Matterhorn of the Himalayas. There were a number of tents at Tapovan. One belonged to a trekking group and another was for a support crew for three American climbers who were scaling a new big wall route on Meru Peak at the head of the valley. They had spent 20 days climbing the huge vertical wall and the support team was quite relieved to see the three climbers stumbling towards camp just before dark in a light sleet storm. They were unsuccessful but had climbed nearly 24 hours nonstop on the descent, since they had run out of food and water. The first climber staggered by carrying a massive haul bag. I said hello as he walked past and his only comment was that he was whipped. I would later find out that the climber was Conrad Anker. We were invited by their liaison officer to share in the group rice and lentil dinner which was much needed as we didn't bring much food ourselves. After dinner, we returned to our makeshift camp and watched a herd of Ibex sheep feeding close by with alpenglow on the snow cliffs above us. The end of the day couldn't have been more majestic.

It was a cold night. A short rain had dampened my shelter and the night air created a layer of ice on top of my sleeping bag. Towards morning the chill had me tossing and turning to stave off the cold, waiting for the sun to rise. I stuck my head out into the frigid air and gazed at the stars. Orion hung in the sky just off the right shoulder of Mt. Shivling. A fading moon's light reflected off the hanging snow and ice thousands of feet above me. I lay there and watched the morning light fill the sky with a soft glow. Within an hour and a half of sunrise, we had packed our camp and were walking back across the glacier to the main trail junction at Gaumukh. I suggested that we visit the river. The loose dirt gave way under my feet, spilling rocks down the slope as I reached the bank and stepped on a flat rock where I could kneel down to touch the cold glacial water. A hundred yards upstream, it rushed out of the bottom of the ice wall. This was the source and headwater of the sacred river Ganges beginning its long journey into the plains of India. I cupped my hands in the frigid water and lifted it up over my head letting the drops fall, wetting my hair. As I walked back along the trail, I passed an elderly man on his own pilgrimage who smiled and said what a happy day this was. I grinned and agreed that yes, this was a happy day. He looked intensely into my eyes and hugged me as he said "Yes, this is a very happy day".

It was fifteen miles of walking back to Gangotri. The scenery and lack of people were signs that the trekking season was coming to an end. My feet were tired after the six and a half hour walk but I was pleased to see Sameer's smiling face and a hot bowl of tomato soup that we consumed quickly before once again crawling into the small diesel car. The rains arrived and soon the road was a mess with large pools of standing water that attempted to drown our car, but at least there were no landslides to deal with during the drive back to Utterkashi. After a short time, we stopped in the village of Harsil and purchased a bag of apples from a road side stand which were delicious and much needed. Once settled in our lodging in Naitala, I enjoyed a hot shower, the first in four days, which I relished.

The next day we were in need of gasoline once again and the first two villages with fuel stations were out of gas. Sameer took a gamble and we took a detour from our route to another small town and we were in luck. Once refueled, we had a slow drive through lovely pine forests. All the undergrowth was eaten by the grazing livestock. With my head out the window, smelling the warm pine scented air, I watched groups of yellow butterflies flapping their wings. The road was lined with the small red flowers. Again, I had a feeling of peace and familiarity. By noon we were hungry and stopped at the lonely Krish Hotel with a staff consisting of a young man, a teenager and a small girl who were quite excited to have paying guests. We enjoyed tea and parathas filled with potato and their garden grown red chilies. Sitting outside at a small table and devouring our lunch, a large rat dashed up the stairs and right between Tim's legs as it disappeared through the hotel door. We just shook our heads and laughed. Nothing is a surprise in India.

Yamunotri

We drove until 3:00 PM following the Yamuna River and arrived at the village of Rana Chatti. The only lodging was a dilapidated hotel and a room with questionable sanitation. The dirty, torn rags that were at one time drapes hung thread bare and the pillow and bed cover looked as if they had never been washed. The electricity went out an hour after we arrived and would reappear randomly with a flicker of hallway lights. I took a two-hour nap in my bivy sack on top of the bed with the hope of sealing out any bug infestation. Dinner was eaten in a tarp roofed hovel across the street. The small wood burning stoves were manned by two cooks. I don't think there is such a thing as food handler permits or health department inspections in rural India so I took my chances with the rice, dal and fried flat bread. Sameer joined us with what he considered a special treat, a chunk of moldy yak butter. He cut off the green parts and plopped a huge chunk in both Tim's and my dal. As I looked down at the melting fat, I kept thinking to myself, "oh please stomach, survive this." Things didn't improve after dinner. As we attempted to go to sleep, a local bus arrived and someone decided to set up a blender outside our door since electricity had been restored. I pushed my ear plugs deeper into my ears and dozed off to the sound of metal grinding.

We only had seven more days in India. It felt like time had stood still. With so many miles, places and people, it was hard to grasp. I had been living moment to moment. We had achieved one objective after another with really only a few days of downtime in Rishikish. I had seen so much of the human condition. I more fully understood the need to have compassion, respect and good will towards others. It was summed up by a conversation I had with a

Yamunotri

manual laborer I had passed along the road. He asked me, "What is the name of your God?" I answered "God." He said, "Mine too."

Sameer had arranged for a jeep to take us the remaining six miles to the trailhead to Yamunotri, our last temple of the Char Dham. But the next morning, we were told that the driver wanted 1,000 rupees vs the 100 we had agreed upon. Sameer believed that he could get us to Yamunotri in his car. Once we started, we realized that the road barely existed. Somehow Sameer's driving skills and his little diesel car delivered us to the trailhead, after a slow hour of driving. We quickly gathered our packs and started walking the trail to the temple.

The mostly paved trail switch backed up Yamuna gorge, a lush valley ringed with waterfalls. When we finally arrived at the temple, it stood claustrophobic in a tight location at the upper end of the valley. As I walked towards the entrance gate, I removed my shoes and gave them to the kneeling attendant. A smiling elderly priest stood at the entrance, and when I handed him my 100-rupee donation he proceeded to bless me. I followed him inside to the altar where he performed a prayer in Hindi and gave me a gift of rice, wrapped in a red and gold fabric which he blessed in front of the idols. He then led us around the altar three times and out the door. This was the last temple of the Char Dahm. I stood for a short time listening to the bells ringing in the distance and the rushing water of the Yamuna River in the cool mountain air. It felt like all things were in their rightful place.

As the day ended, we drove back along the same horrible road to the same horrible hotel. We pleaded to Sameer to find some other lodging, and with a smile, he offered to drive us the six hours to Mussoorie and the hill country. It was only 1:00 PM.

As we entered a small village, I watched as three children played and laughed, splashing water on a tired looking water buffalo standing in the middle of a concrete water trough. The countryside slowly passed by. Sameer honked his horn as we crossed a rise, as is the practice, but instead of an oncoming vehicle several cows stood in the middle of the road. With the honking of the horn the cows took off at a run. Suddenly, out of the trees a woman and a small girl appeared. It was their livestock we had just spooked. We drove down the road herding the cattle toward an opening in a fence and were able to move them from the center of the road into a field. The woman and child ran up behind us and quickly disappeared behind their cows.

The sun had heated the pine trees so their fragrance filled the air. Sameer played a tape of Hindi music and with the windows rolled down and warm sun on our skin, we bobbed to the music. Tim and I sipped on cold beer and ate salted peanuts that Sameer had bought in a shop at the first village we had passed. Tim proposed a toast, "To a fitting end to our Char Dham. And as George Peppard of the TV show The A Team would say, 'I love it when a plan comes together.'" Sameer congratulated us.

Mussoorie

The remaining journey to Mussoorie, known as Queen of the Hills, was up a twisting road that climbed into the clouds. During the 1800's, the British Army used the hill stations as an escape from the heat of the plains. Mussoorie was one of those respites. After a long day, all we wanted was a clean place to sleep and some decent food. We were in luck since the town was bustling in preparation of the Hindu holiday, Dussehra. Mussoorie is known for its beautiful setting and a waterfall known as Kempy Falls, jokingly called the Niagara Falls of India for the numbers of honeymooners. I slept through the variety of sounds that came through the thin walls and dreamt the vivid dreams that had been my constant companion night after night.

The primary goal for the next morning was to find and visit Hathipaon Park Estate of Sir George Everest, the Surveyor General of India during the mid-1800's. Sameer asked several locals for directions and after some effort we found the correct road which ended in a washout about a mile from the site and six miles from Mussoorie. We walked the uneven road to a large white mansion that sat at the top of a knoll on a ridge. The views were magnificent with the lush valley floor was covered in a rising mist. Cattle grazed on the terraced lawns. The stucco walls of the main building were in wonderful condition and the roof remained intact even though it was built in the 1830's. I wandered through the open entry. Graffiti covered many of the walls but the building had such an air of history. Each room had a built-in fireplace and I imagined them lit and sputtering as the rains of the monsoons hammered the house. Wandering out the back of the building and up a small hill stood another structure that was Everest's observatory, providing a view of the estate's grounds. I sat and wrote with my back against a tall wall and enjoyed the beauty of the location. Nearby was a low cement slab that, according to Tim, was the last point of the Great Trigonometrical Survey of India.

Above the main house was a low hill with rows and rows of prayer flags. I went for a closer look and was in awe. As I arrived, the wind increased and hundreds of colorful flags lifted into the air, tugging at the cord that kept them earth bound. The sound of the flags flapping filled the air. A powerful chill ran through my body and I was filled with joy. I found a flat rock to sit on and with the sun on my face and the sound of the flags filling the air, a small orange and black butterfly landed on my knee. Butterflies have become my companions on this journey. An outcropping of black rock created a high stage behind me and as I turned my head, I saw several large monkeys sitting on the crest staring at me. A blue prayer flag lay on the ground. I reached down and picked it up and walked over to a string of flags within my reach. I tied the flag to the line and made a wish for luck and happiness.

Back in Mussoorie, we went to a bar for a few drinks. I made a comment about how I was blown away by the prayer flags at the Everest House. Tim just shook his head at my unintentional pun. We wandered to the main square for the grand finale of the Dussehra festival. As we left the cafe, we were passed by a wedding procession. A cart with a large amplifying system was being pushed down the street, followed by a brass band. The wedding group was segregated, with the groom and males of the party dancing behind the band, and the females walking behind, very proper and subdued.

After the wedding party passed, we walked to the main square where a 20-foot-tall wood and paper figure stood. It was Ravana, the 10-headed Hindu king of the demons. The square was packed with people and young men threw firecrackers onto the pavement creating huge sparks that flew up and bounced off of bystanders. I patted out several sparks that burned holes straight through my jacket. After a procession carrying people dressed as Lord Rama a Hindu deity and his disciple Lord Hanuman, the large figure of Ravana was set on fire. The flames rose dramatically into the night sky.

I stood next to a very large man with the traditional turban and beard of a Sikh. We talked and I relayed my experience of bathing at Hemkund and was immediately adopted by him. My beard and long hair may have helped break the ice. He introduced me to his family of three sons, their wives and his brother. He kept hugging

Hathipaon

me and referred to me as brother. The family was quite excited to meet me and impressed with my Hemkund visit. I had had such wonderful interactions with Sikhs and I treasured meeting him and his family. I had been able to experience some amazing interactions with Hindus, Buddhist, Sikhs and Christians. The devout are all the same, at least the open-hearted ones.

Homeward

Our time in India was coming to a close. While driving back to Dehra Dun we stopped at a Shri Sai Babba temple and received a blessing by the local priest. That was followed by a quick stop

Temple Bells

at Sahastradhara to visit a cave which had been transformed into a place of worship and once again we were given a blessing. In the Tibetan community of Dehra Dun was the Og Min Ogyen Mindrolling Monastery and the Great Peace Stupa where we stopped and spent the latter part of the afternoon. We were fortunate to arrive while a performance of Tibetan male dancers was underway. We sat on the floor and watched the elaborately clothed performers rotating in slow circles. It was a welcome rest from the noise and traffic.

Our last night in India would be one of heavy drinking in a seedy bar named 'Bar' that had us worse for wear on the drive back to New Delhi. After hours of driving, we stopped at a small village where Sameer saw his uncle on a motorcycle who invited us for a soda. We stopped in front of a small roadside shack that sold soft drinks and tea. The small shop was crammed with men from the village, hardworking laborers. At first, I felt uncomfortable, especially with one rather menacing man staring straight at me. Sameer made a few jokes and the harsh stares turned to laughter. I was thankful again to see the good in people.

As we approached the outskirts of Delhi, I caught a last glimpse of the rural landscape. The sun was setting and with the typical air pollution the sky was a wonderful soft orange gauze. I felt incredibly sad to be leaving this strange place. Overcome with feelings of a past life lived here and an unexplained strong connection and love for India.

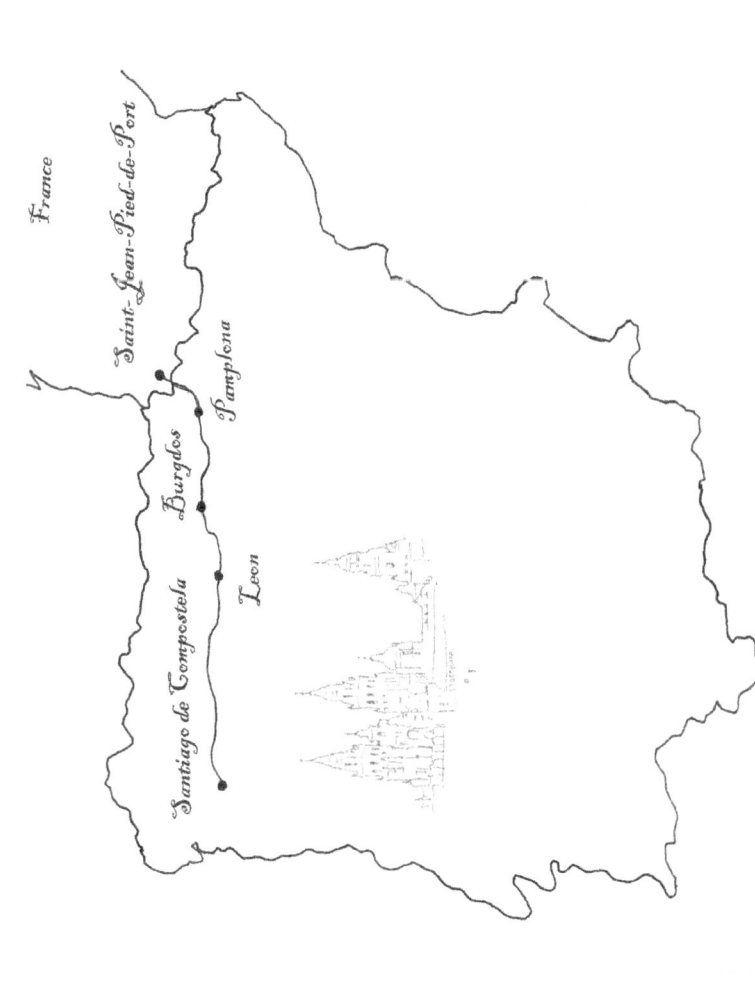

France

Saint-Jean-Pied-de-Port

Pamplona

Burgdos

Leon

Santiago de Compostela

Camino de Santiago,
Meditation by Feet on the Way of St. James

The Camino de Santiago (Way of St. James) pilgrimage dates back to the 8th Century. The normal route begins in St. Jean Pied de Port, France and ends nearly 500 miles later in Santiago de Compostela, Spain. After successfully completing the Hindu Char Dham and Buddhist Kailash pilgrimages, I became committed to traveling to France and Spain to walk the ancient Catholic Camino.

The plan came together rather quickly. My friend and mountaineering partner, Tim, decided to come along after my daughter cornered him and insisted that he join me on the walk to watch over me. An over protective daughter, especially endearing since she used to call me "O.P."

2011 was a year of personal loss. My friend Suzanne died in a mountaineering accident in Alaska, my stepmother succumbed to cancer, and our two dogs died months apart. Another acquaintance, with whom I had gone on multiple ski trips, passed away from complications after a routine surgery, and I still mourned my 98-year-old grandfather who had died the year before. I began to view the pilgrimage as a way of coming to terms with my grief. Although I was nervous about the number of miles to be walked, I jumped into the deep end of the pool once again.

Tim on the Road

The Pilgrimage

I met Tim at the gate in Seattle for our British Airways flight to Chicago. It went smoothly, and we arrived with plenty of time for pizza and beer. We boarded the flight to London which was a half hour late and sat on the plane for another hour and a half while a thunderstorm and flashes of lightning passed overhead. I was seated next to a young woman from Prague who was flying home to visit family, and as the time passed, we both began to worry about our connecting flights. Suddenly a hail storm began to pound the outside of the plane and we were de-boarded. All the planes that could have sustained hail damage needed to be inspected. Our flight was delayed for five hours.

Arriving in London, we got in line for boarding passes since the front desk in Chicago was not able to print them. We still had 45 minutes until our flight but the computer system would not print the passes since we didn't have enough time to get through security. Our only option was to rebook a later flight.

We finally arrived in Paris but missed our flight from Paris to Biarritz. By now, we were exhausted and numb as we wandered through the airport trying to figure how to make it to the south of France. There were no trains or flights until the next morning. We contemplated renting a car and driving the nine hours to southern France. We could take a chance and try to get on the only direct EasyJet flight at 7:00 AM without a reservation (and another 175 Euros each) or take a train from the Montparnasse train station in central Paris. We had a conversation with a staff member at the tourist information center and were dissuaded from driving or flying. He gave us a business card for an inexpensive hotel that had a free shuttle from the airport, so we rented a room to get some sleep and a much-needed shower.

The next morning, we were up and in the lobby before 5:00 and requested a cab to the train station. We were informed that no taxis were available and we would have to take the shuttle back to the airport. Once back at the airport we grabbed a taxi that took us into Paris at sunrise and left us at the Montparnasse train station. We found the ticket office which was just opening and asked for a ticket to Bayonne but their computer system was down so we were told to go to the train platform, board the train and buy a ticket once on board. We tried that but were told we couldn't stay onboard without a ticket. I attempted to buy two tickets through a kiosk but it would not take my credit card, so we went back to the start and were able to buy two tickets to Bayonne at the ticket office. We finally boarded the high speed TVG train for the five-hour trip to Bayonne. We joked that walking 500 miles would be easier than all the effort just to get to the start of the Camino. Tim pointed to his Saint Bernard medal that my daughter Hillary had given him and said, "this guy isn't helping at all." I realized this was a pilgrimage, but I was already exhausted.

The high-speed train sped south past bright yellow and green fields. The train was comfortable and after several trips to the dining car for beer we had forgotten the last two days of flying. Reaching Bayonne was a relief. We easily found the hotel where our other two hiking partners, Mike and Greg, were already checked in, and after a quick shower, we toured Bayonne with its houses painted white with dark red trim and orange tiled roofs.

We entered a small bar and were welcomed by a large Frenchman in a soccer jersey who spoke fluent English. Bayonne had won the local soccer championship and people were celebrating the victory. As we stood in a circle near the bar, we were joined by an elderly man who didn't speak English. The group welcomed him and I was told that he had fought with the French Resistance during WWII and that his brother had been captured and died in a German concentration camp. I told our English-speaking friend that six of my uncles had fought in the war and two had been in France. He translated what I'd said to the old man who reached over, shook my hand and bought me a beer in appreciation for my family's service. It meant a lot to me.

The next morning, we packed and headed to the train station for an 8:30 AM departure to St. Jean Pied de Port, but a trestle bridge over a river had collapsed a few days prior to our arrival so buses were arranged, another blip in our continuing travel saga. Arriving in St. Jean, we found the Camino office and got our pilgrim's passports and a shell for our packs to identify us as pilgrims. St. Jean is a lovely ancient village with cobblestone streets in an idyllic setting. The four of us were referred to a hostel just out of town that sat alone on a grass covered hill with spectacular views over French farmlands.

The Start

I didn't sleep well, so I was awake and standing on the veranda at 4:00 AM to watch the sun rise. The valley was filled with fog and as the sun turned the sky orange, there was an amazing symphony of bird song that gradually replaced the silence. I was cold but couldn't leave their beautiful performance. After a simple breakfast, we began walking the Route de Napoleon up and over the Pyrenees mountains into Spain. The weather was beautiful. The road meandered through lush farmland and soon we passed a decaying building with a large rose bush that reached towards the tile roof. Several red roses bloomed against the white washed wall. Further along, as the road climbed, we passed white sheep grazing and newly tilled brown fields under cobalt blue skies. The road transitioned to a narrow path ending at the top of a ridge where we stopped and rested. The view was magnificent across multiple peaks and valleys. There was a small statue of the Virgin Mary. Several female pilgrims began to sing, "Maria, I just met a girl named Maria." Tim joked that the hills were indeed alive with the sound of music.

We walked through open countryside until we reached a beech forest - one of the last remaining in Europe. The footpath widened and was covered with rust-colored leaves. My feet bounced on top of the organic cushion as gusts of wind lifted the dryer leaves as if the ground had come alive. I felt the curve and weight of my pack. I thought of my friend Suzanne, knowing she had worn the pack I now carried. She handmade it for the Pacific Northwest Trail thru-hike and had carried it for over a month as one of the first hikers. That thought comforted me as I completed my first day of the Camino.

We reached the pass, Col de Lepoeder, and took shelter from the wind in a dip in the ground. A German woman hunkered down next to us and the five of us lay on our backs on the grass, away from the cold wind, letting the sun warm our bodies. The descent into the valley was steep and slick but the sunlight filtered through the beech leaves and I no longer felt as tired as I had earlier. We arrived at the alberque in Roncesvalles. A long day, the first of many to come.

Scallop Shell

Witches

The next morning, we were walking in the dark along a wooded path that ran parallel to a paved road. Clouds only added to the early morning darkness and within an hour it began to rain. We started walking with a young Italian man in bright orange running shoes. Just as we left the heavy woods, we passed a stone cross. A sign informed us that witch covens held forbidden rituals at this spot and were later executed here. A spine-chilling place to be in the rain and dark.

The relentless rain made our path muddy for most of the 17 miles of walking. We crossed a large boggy pasture and then headed steeply down, crossing the Rio Arga at Zubiri. I found a market and purchased a coke and snack and sat under a roof overhang out of the worst of the day's downpour, and removed my rain-soaked poncho. Though it was cold it was nice to take off the wet nylon for a short time and rest.

Our destination for the day was the Larrasoana alberque. We arrived and had to wait a couple of hours to check in. It was a lengthy process to get registered as each pilgrim's name, travel passport number and country of origin had to be handwritten into a large binder. Each Camino passport was stamped and a payment collected. This was the registration process at all alberques.

Larrasoana is a very small village with one bar and store. The bar is the social gathering spot of all the pilgrims. We were lucky to get a large table and shared it with the Italian with the orange shoes and his German friend, as well as two American and two Swedish women.

Burst of Yellow

The morning routine was getting established. We woke up early and were walking by 6:00, usually the first ones to leave, always in the dark with headlamps. We had 13 miles to cover that day with a lot of up and down. The first several miles of the hike were through farmland, much of it along a lovely wooded river. The tranquil countryside changed as we approached the outskirts of Pamplona. The path turned into miles of pavement through suburbs and business districts until we reached a park like setting and the great walled city. Entering the ancient city, we walked along narrow cobblestone streets and time worn buildings just as one would expect in old Spain. I had read Ernest Hemingway's The Sun Also Rises, about the famous running of the bulls that is held every July, and pictured myself running down a narrow alley with thundering hooves in pursuit.

We continued on through the afternoon heat to Cizur Menor. The Camino followed a busy highway with no shade, but I didn't mind the heat, walking beside the bright yellow canola fields to our alberque for the night. The yellow burst against the blue sky - a moving artist's palette.

Illumination

The next day started with mugs of instant coffee. Even simple pleasures were wonderful on this arduous trek. It was still dark as we walked into the sunrise. The terrain changed from woodlands to open farmland. The wheat fields were golden and shimmering. Our path climbed a dirt track towards a ridge line of wind turbines. Red poppies bloomed along the trail providing a bright exclamation of color. Once we reached the high point, Alto del Perdon, we took a short rest behind a metal sculpture of pilgrims on their way to Santiago before heading down the path into the next valley.

Mike and Tim took off at a fast pace so I took my time walking with a young German. We all met up at the edge of the village of Muruzabal and decided to take a detour to Eunate to visit the eight-sided church of the Knights Templar from the 12th Century. The church sat alone just off a busy highway. The arched entrance led to a walled inner keep and heavy wooden doors that stood open. We entered the darkened interior and our eyes adjusted to reveal simple wooden pews and a carved statue of Maria de Eunate. A bus arrived and the tour guide put a coin in a meter and illuminated the small statue. The elderly Spanish tourists let out a communal sigh. The guide then led them in a hymn. I stood in the back, listening to their beautiful voices. The windows were inlayed with a thin white stone which let in a very soft light. It was a beautiful moment.

Echoes of Prayer and Worship

The next morning was perfectly cool as we walked in the dark. I loved seeing the moon every day before sunrise. As we continued walking for the next month, I was able to enjoy all of its phases from new to full. Each morning as the sun rose, a concert of bird song filled the air, singing their welcome to another day. The mornings were a highlight of the journey.

We covered 13 miles that day and even though I was still getting in walking shape it went fairly well. Partway, we walked along a short section of a 2,000-year-old Roman road, dropping down a short hill and over a stream. The Roman stonework and arch over the water were in beautiful condition, well worth a short break and a few photos. We hiked for another four hours before stopping at the abandoned church of San Miquel. A grove of olive trees grew above knee-high weeds. There were a few picnic tables where we sat and took off our boots. The church was open and its interior was stripped bare except for a huge wooden cross and a table covered in offerings and notes from passing pilgrims. The church had the same feel as one I had visited in Argentina in the 1980's during a climbing expedition to Aconcagua, austere but full of echoes of prayer and worship. As we headed down through vineyards to Estella, the soil changed to bright red clay.

Fountain of Wine

I awoke at 5:00 after a long night of strange, unsettling dreams. It took some time to find our way out of Estella and into the countryside in the dark. Our first stop was at the Monastery Irache and the Fuente de Vino (the fountain of wine). Even though it was still before sunrise, we purchased a small glass from the vending machine and sampled the free-flowing wine. The wine was not too bad even at that time of the morning. As the sun rose, we were treated to miles of wheat fields. A cool breeze blew over the green sea. The ripples and waves of the flowing wheat were magical. It reminded me of my childhood in northwestern Nebraska. The hot sun bore down on me and my boots were covered in dust. I found I was starting to want to walk alone, giving me time to think. The days were becoming easier.

Our track passed through a lengthy section of small trees before arriving at Villamayor de Monjardin and the ruins of a castle that sit on a hill above the village. We stopped and had espresso at a rather new alberque with outside tables. It had a hippy vibe with a mural patio. I got in trouble with the owner's wife as I thought the blue concrete structure with running water in the back garden area was a place where I could do my laundry. Turns out it was a small fountain. She was not happy.

Rioja

The next day was long. The morning walk went up and over a couple of steep hills before flattening for miles on a red dirt track through open wheat fields and vineyards. The scenery was serene, and an overcast sky and cool breeze made the hiking pleasant. Tim commented about how many ants he saw crossing the trail at many places along the way. He called them Tiny Pilgrims.

We left the province of Navarra and entered Rioja. Our first and only rest stop that day was in the village of Viana. A row of cafes lined the narrow street in front of the cathedral of Iglesia Santa Maria where pilgrims from many countries sat relaxing and laughing. I visited the cathedral and sat alone and prayed.

The last few miles from Viana to Logrono were incredibly painful. As we walked down the steep pavement, I began to get shin splints. The miles stretched on, with each step filling my legs with pain. I finally made it to the alberque in Logrono. After eating lunch, I rested for the afternoon and evening. I was worried that I might not be able to continue. The remaining journey seemed daunting.

Wheat to Wine

Clear skies and a gentle breeze greeted us as we walked with headlamps out of Logrono. The day's route was nearly 19 miles on a flat track. At sunrise we passed Lake Planano de la Grajera. Fishermen stood shoulder to shoulder along the shore beneath ancient gnarled trees. We were treated to the sight of a native squirrel with its brown furry coat and white chest.

Eventually, the wheat fields gave way to vineyards. The red clay earth of Rioja with its stunted ancient grape vines was so dramatic with the always blue sky breaking the horizon. I sat on a small concrete block, drank water and breathed in the moment. As the day went on my shin splints ached but I persevered to Najera.

Campos de Trigo

Meditation with Feet

The next day's start was quick as the temperature was quite cool. It helped us cover the first few miles at a rapid pace until we found a café that was serving espresso. It tasted wonderful. The remainder of the day's walk meandered up and down through the rural setting except for one long stretch where the road reached out before us as far as we could see. The road turned into a trail lined with a chain link fence. Crosses had been woven into the fence with sticks made of wood. Symbols of reverence appeared even in the most mundane places.

Before noon, we arrived at a golf resort in what seemed to be the middle of nowhere. The green course was surrounded by multi-level condo buildings which had window after window of "For Sale" signs. A few bottom floor units looked inhabited as the small front lawns were manicured and flowing with flowers. One large complex was a shell of concrete, the result of the real estate boom in Spain collapsing. The money just ran out.

The day's 13-mile walk ended in Santo Domingo de la Calzada. We arrived shortly before the alberque opened so with our packs placed in queue we wandered to a nearby tapas bar for a cold beer and snack. My favorite was white asparagus wrapped in ham with a dab of hollandaise sauce on a toasted piece of bread. One of the patrons bought us a small glass of sweet dessert wine which complimented the tapas very well. That little snack was the most delicious food so far on the journey.

Once we got our beds, I showered and took a nap until 2:00 when we were told that a procession was about to begin at the cathedral. Most of the local residents stood outside the massive church doors. A group of teenage boys dressed in berets and traditional costumes stood nervously clicking their castanets. The doors opened and the elders carried a large statue of a saint on their shoulders. The procession began. The dancing youth led the troupe, then the saint, followed by a brass band. I found a good spot to watch and enjoyed our luck at arriving on this special day in Domingo de la Calzada. This is the third pilgrimage I had been on. I thought that I would experience the same emotional sensations as in India but I hadn't. India seemed so personal, full of déjà vu and familiar as if another life had been spent there. Here, I had spent much time in my own thoughts. A meditation with feet. Something had changed in me, but it was subtle.

Shell and Boots

Red Clay

The next morning, a sliver of a moon hung in the sky as we walked into the Province of Leon from Rioja. The vineyards diminished and the fields turned once again to wheat. Red clay earth changed back to brown. The few small villages we walked through were asleep. As the sun rose, two jet contrails formed a cross in the orange sky. I looked up and acknowledged the sign with a silent thank you.

The track merged onto the shoulder of a busy highway for miles. It was a shock to our senses. We were happy to cover the fifteen miles and stop at the first alberque outside Belorado. It was a privately run lodge and pleasantly only had a few bunk beds per room. Outside was a grassy picnic area with a swimming pool. With a cold beer at my side, I sat with my feet in the cool pool water. Tim stripped down to his shorts and dove in. The sun was hot and I laid back and melted into the grass as Mike struggled with his blistered feet. We all needed a rest.

The Fallen

The moon was in its new phase, so the early morning departure through the dark streets of Belorado was challenging. We were confused as we scoured the sidewalks, street signs and buildings for the yellow arrows or shells that marked the Camino. We eventually arrived at the main track of the Way and entered the countryside once again. The trail then steadily climbed into an oak forest with distant views of snow-covered peaks and hillsides of wind generators that rose above the fog that lay thick in the valley.

Once on the ridge, the trail climbed up and over three high points. The ridge seemed never ending and my feet were tired, but it was a beautiful day and my energy was good. I took a short rest at a tall wooden cross at the top of one of the high points (Cruz de Madera) and another at the monument to Los Caidos (the fallen of the Spanish Civil War of 1936). We arrived in San Juan de Ortega after 15 miles of walking. Inside the local church, I sat down and took some time alone, to think and regroup. It was pleasant in the cool stone interior, away from my hiking companions.

Cows in the Mist

Another typical morning, and after walking for an hour, the sunrise gave us light as we passed through an oak and pine forest with trunks covered in layers of moss that hung thick and wet. I stopped at one point and took a photo with my old Rollei camera of the rising sun through the fog and heavy morning dew that dripped from the grass. Thoughts filled my day as I walked the 16 miles to Burgos. I reaffirmed my thankfulness for my wife Beck and daughter Hillary and the love I have for them. I vowed to keep the people who have died recently alive by remembering them. I would simplify my life, or at least try. I would nurture friendships and not let them slip away as I have done so many times before.

Slowly, cows began to appear out of the mist. The sky lightened and the sun illuminated a village in a green valley below. We dropped down, then back up steeply, reaching another stoic cross marking the top of a hill. From there we could look down onto the sprawling city of Burgos.

It took a couple of hours to drop down to the outskirts and actually arrive at the city center. On the way, the trail split and we took a route that led us around the airport and past the city landfill and an area of graffiti covered buildings - the worst section of walking on the whole Camino.

There was plenty of time to relax in Burgos with its shops, dining options and sightseeing. The immense cathedral was inspiring. We walked around the perimeter and using our Pilgrims Passport where were given a discount on the entrance fee. The interior of the church was expansive. The arches soared upwards, reaching for the heavens.

The Snails

The next morning, we again had a difficult time finding our way out of town in the early hours. The overcast skies shortly turned to rain and I had to drop my backpack and pull out my rain poncho. The downpour lasted for about an hour, stopped, then started again as each squall rolled in. We passed a tree-lined river that was quite tranquil with rain drops breaking the water's surface. With the dampness came tiny snails that began to fill the pathway. There was no way to avoid the crackle of their shells underfoot as the narrow path was bordered by high vegetation. I was distressed by their deaths. I noticed the stork nests built on the top of nearby chimneys. Their huge hanging nests formed islands of sticks above our heads. Beautiful red roses grew up a white washed wall of a small house. The roses and several groups of large purple irises alleviated some of the distress over the death of the snails.

In four hours, we covered the 12 miles to Hornillos. After dinner, I walked over to the side of the church to watch the sunset through the layers of grey clouds. It turned into a circle of intense color. I clung to the moment and savored the Spanish light.

Plains of Wheat

The alberque was small and noisy. I lay awake much of the night until I rustled the others for an early exit. We hiked a road in the pitch black and as it entered the countryside, morning arrived. We crested the hilltop onto the flat of the meseta (plains) with wheat fields stretching as far as I could see. The lonely dirt road split the expanse as it disappeared into the distance.

It began to rain and the wet slog began. The passing squalls had us reaching for our ponchos yet again. The red clay stuck to the bottom of our boots, several inches thick. After three hours we finally came across a hamlet hidden in the bottom of a small hollow. It was wonderful to take a rest inside a café where it was warm and dry, sipping hot coffee. With a lot of mental effort our damp clothing was gathered and once again we ventured out into the rain. The hike through the valley improved once the rain stopped and birds began to sing.

After a few miles, we came across the abandoned ruins of the San Anton convent. A grand arch spanned the road with broken stone walls. It was roofless and stone pieces littered the interior. It felt like it had been a special place. I found a large stone section of fallen wall that lay sideways on the ground. It provided a rest spot and I sat. A stork had built a nest at the top of one of the walls and its head would occasionally appear and gaze down at me. History surrounded me.

It was a short day to Castrojeriz and its castle. We were only two days from the half way point and as a whole, things were going quite well.

Rough Edges

There was no moon the next morning so headlamps were essential. The yellow arrows quickly led us out of town and onto a dirt road that once again climbed upwards. The track over the last few weeks had gained and lost a lot of elevation so it was just more of the same. We gained 600 feet before sunrise and the lights of Castrojeriz showed how far we had climbed. Once we arrived at the top of the hill, we faced a strong bitterly cold wind. There was a three-sided stone shelter that was built specifically for pilgrims. I put on all my additional clothing and faced the wind. I walked quickly to try and stay warm and soon outpaced the others.

Once again, the scenery of the Meseta lay flat and expansive. No villages were in sight but after some time another small jewel of a valley appeared with a few buildings and we were able to purchase a much-needed coffee and pastry. The fuel revived my energy and after another few miles I stopped for a second coffee. The hills and terrain reminded me so much of Nebraska, flat and green. We followed a canal bank (Canal de Castilla) for a few miles and once again I was transported to my Midwest childhood. Tall reeds grew along the water's edge and were filled with songbirds singing their individual songs.

We crossed over a bridge on the Rio Pisuerga and left the province of Burgos and entered Palencia. An old woman walked by and wished me a "Buen Camino." The people in the villages are supportive of pilgrims walking to Santiago de Compostela and occurred often. We arrived in Fromista around 11:30 AM, having covered nearly 16 miles in six hours of walking, and had several hours to wait until the alberque opened. We found a bar and ordered pizza and beer. I burnt my fingers on the hot plate, even though I'd been told not to touch it.

It was a beautiful evening so we walked to the Mercado and purchased red wine, cheese, chorizo, bread, pimentos, and white asparagus. Sitting in the main square were the two American women who we had met earlier, their Australian friend and a crazy cigarette smoking German who waved us over to join them. It was an enjoyable evening sitting in the warmth of the sun with newly found friends. I said a 'Kim-ism,' my friend Tim's name for my crazy sayings, that had everyone laughing. "This beer did a pretty good job of smoothing out the rough edges, whatever rough edges I've got."

Canal de Castilla

Carrion De Los Condes – The Nuns

The next morning the unsettled weather seemed to have passed. With clear skies, the day's hike was along a rough rocky path next to a highway. At the first village the group split, with me taking the shorter route beside the busy asphalt road. Though my path had deafening traffic noise it was nice to be alone. The trek to Carrion De Los Condes ended at the Parish alberque which is run by nuns. They were wonderful. They gave each of us a small religious medallion and showed us to our clean room with single beds arranged throughout the large sleeping area. This was the first night since the beginning of the walk we didn't have to sleep in bunk beds. It was a treat.

The open-air courtyard was a pleasant spot to do hand laundry, read, and write in my journal under a warm sun with large storks and their chaotic nests sitting overhead. The nuns have some strict rules. A young man sitting in the courtyard removed his shirt to enjoy the sun. It wasn't long before one of the sisters rushed over and gave him quite the lecture as he quickly pulled his shirt back over his head.

Terradillos de los Templarios

We had hoped to get an early start in the morning but the nuns keep the exit doors locked until 6:00 AM. It was 6:30 before we were walking out of town. I had plenty of energy since the day before had been relaxing and I'd had a good night's sleep, after not much wine drinking. I kept a fast, steady pace all day on the nearly flat trail which allowed me the pleasure of hiking alone. My mind wandered through a long list of issues. Hours melted together as my path merged onto an ancient Roman road, perfectly engineered in its straightness. There were fewer songbirds but now and then one would appear for a short performance. Eventually, a village appeared and I was able to get a boost from some weak coffee.

We finished the days 17 mile walk in five hours. Terradillos de los Templarios has a population of 80 and no cafes or mercados but one lovely private alberque in which we were able to book a room for the four of us with a private bathroom for nine euros each. We had the whole afternoon to spend sitting in the sun, doing hand laundry in the outside sink, sipping red wine and devouring several bowls of large olives. I spent the day in reflection and realized I could forgive myself for past transgressions.

Calzadilla de los Hermanillos

The night's sleep ended after a long dream that I was pleased to be released from. We were dressed, packed and walking by 6:00 AM in the near pitch dark. Tim disappeared in the distance and Greg disappeared to the rear with Mike and I walking together until sunrise, where we were joined by a young man who talked nonstop. Both of us just nodded and grunted in our half-asleep, caffeine-deprived state.

Finally, a village appeared with a small café and the smell of coffee and baked pastries. After eating, we parted with our talkative companion and merged onto a flat, dirt path through plowed fields. The dirt road to Calzadilla de los Hermanillos was dusty and hot with no shade. The eight miles were demanding. We were walking on one of the oldest Roman military roads in Spain. The smooth stones were very difficult to walk on, forcing us to tread along the road's edge. We saw no one and I began to think that maybe we had taken the wrong turn. A village eventually appeared. We were able to eat a large lunch with a Spanish pilgrim who we had seen every other day or so since we crossed into Spain.

The day had been beautiful with a sunrise feast of orange and red, a field of lavender with its intense purple color, the warmth of the sun on my back, and a bench in the shade with a flock of swallows performing a lovely dance of flight around me.

No One is Ever Alone on the Camino

Our walk started before 6:30 AM on a nice flat section of road. I stopped at a stand of stunted pine trees and listened to the birds' songs rise to a crescendo as sunrise woke the earth. After the pine grove the path merged onto another ancient Roman stone road (Calzada Romana) that stretched into the distance. Mundane scenery and walking for hours lulled me into a stupor until I was rudely awakened by a speeding train that came out of nowhere. At least it prompted us to stop for a lunch. Sitting on the ground, I enjoyed my salami, bread and salted nuts but the heat was rising fast. The sun was blazing and my ankle began to ache as we walked along a flat white gravel road that led into town and the end of our 15 miles. We had some time before the alberque opened and nearby was a café which served cold beer and tapas. It gave us some time to regroup and once the doors opened to our nights lodging, I was able to take a welcome shower and catch up on washing my clothes. It felt wonderful to be clean.

We had a nice communal dinner. A young woman who was walking the Camino solo had suffered a large number of bug bites and was quite upset. Several pilgrims at the alberque calmed her, helped with washing her clothes and provided salve to relieve the itching. One of the attendants, a young woman, was especially nice and kept reminding the woman that no one is ever alone on the Camino. All pilgrims walking to Santiago are family, under God's watch.

Leon

The path to Leon was only 11.5 miles and primarily along a busy highway. The only highlight of the walk was the stand of cottonwood trees that had gone to seed, filling the air with white fluff. I noticed a small yard that looked as if it had recently snowed due to the seeds covering the ground. It only took a few hours to reach Leon and as the municipal alberque was still closed for repairs we were able to find one run by the Benedictines (Santa Maria de las Carbajalas). It had three floors of large open rooms with rows and rows of bunk beds.

We had time to explore the city, and since it was Saturday and market day, we wandered between the colorful vendor stalls of fruits, vegetables, flowers, antiques and household items.

The massive cathedral is one of the most beautiful churches in Spain. The interior of the Leon Cathedral was dark and overwhelming in scale. The soaring heights and rows of stained glass filled me with emotions; sadness, inspiration, joy and reverence. I stood in the quiet dim light gazing up at the blue, red and green stained glass, amazed. I found a wooden pew and sat for quite some time, not thinking but just feeling.

I had passed a small wine shop earlier so I headed back and ordered a Rose wine, chilled and delicious. Mike, Tim and Greg eventually found me and I bought them one as well. Mike stayed on and we sampled several local reds recommended by the woman working behind the bar. We tasted some wonderful wines, some of the best so far.

After dinner we sat in the cathedral's main square with new friends and watched the numerous finely dressed wedding parties line up one after another to enter the cathedral for their wedding services. I decided that at some point I would like to return to Leon.

I was very tired of communal sleeping. I lost one of my earplugs during the night and the snoring and heat had me ready to gather my belongings and move outside to a bench in the square. Mike made a comment about how he hated communal sleeping when he was in the Army and how he hated it still.

Leon

Karma and Tara

The alberque gates were locked until 6:00 AM so we had a late start. It took two hours of walking to leave Leon and its suburbs, but we were able to find a small cafe for a quick coffee and a brioche which I needed desperately. Once at the edge of town, our path split with one route following the highway and the other wandering off into the countryside. We took the country route which alternated between dirt road, rocky path and pavement. One of the first villages was one of the prettiest places I had seen in days with its old stone buildings behind a row of cottonwood trees and a small brook. Beyond the town we hiked through a stand of small stunted trees and a field of wild lavender. Further along I watched a hawk fly low overhead looking for prey as it circled a wheat field with a solitary stone cross. Suddenly, it dropped to the ground catching its day's meal.

The rest of the day and evening followed the usual routine; check in, shower, laundry, large meal, nap, wine hour in the afternoon sun, light snack for dinner and to bed. My mind wandered to my two dogs who both had died over the last year. I really missed both of them. Memories of Karma laying stretched out over my chest as I lay on the couch, nuzzling his head against my chin and Tara as she dashed down the hallway chasing a small ball I had just thrown. The two of them were like an old married couple. It wasn't long after Karma died, at over 14 years of age, that Tara seemed to just give up, dying peacefully in her sleep. It still made me sad.

Releasing of Ghosts

The day's walk was over 18 miles. The usual early start and level path along a paved road had me covering the first nine miles in three hours. The four of us reached Hopital del Orbigo on a beautiful late morning and we walked across the famous stone bridge, Passo Honroso (Honourable Crossing) where in the Middle Ages, the knight Don Suero defeated 300 challengers in jousting matches. The town was quite charming and I wished I had the extra time to stay a day but the distant goal of Santiago overrode the desire to stop.

Leaving the village, we climbed to the day's high point of Alto Santa Toribio and its large stone cross. We still had four miles to Astorga. The route headed down a new cobblestone road, through the outskirts to the main square where we found the alberque. I spent the rest of the day taking photographs, writing in my journal, visiting the main cathedral and sipping chilled rose wine in a small bar. I finally felt as though I was getting in shape.

I had many thoughts about my grandfather. It had been a year and a half since he passed. I reran memories of my visits to his small apartment that was attached to my father's aircraft hangar, where he lived after my grandmother passed away and sold the family farm in Nebraska. He would always have a pot of coffee at the ready. We would sit and discuss subject after subject and I would listen to his stories, some repeated several times over the years. He lived until 98 years of age and remained sharp to the end. I missed him. This walk put me in a place where I could not push away thoughts and feelings of friends and family who had died the last couple of years. The days were spent walking in silence except with the ongoing conversations in my head. It felt like a long, slow purging and releasing of ghosts.

Suzanne

With two coffee breaks, I finished the day's walk in a little over four hours. The countryside changed once again and the rolling hills covered with stunted trees were pleasant. The flat trail cut through the hills and the small paved road next to us had few cars. The sunrise outside of Murias de Rechivalso bathed the scenery in golden soft light. The first rest break was at a small village with the only bar being a strange transplant for some other world called the "Cowboy Bar". A boisterous character stood behind the bar in a leather vest and slid our drinks down the bar just like in an old television western. The interior was decorated with cowboy paraphernalia from Spain, Argentina and the US. It was one of those places that you stumble upon, unique and full of weirdness.

We arrived in Rabanal before noon so I had time to explore the few sights. I wandered into a small church and sat for a time. The church radiated reverence and sacredness. I had checked email at the alberque. There was a message that Dave, my dear friend Suzanne's boyfriend, had reached the summit of Denali the day before, the same day Suzanne had perished on the mountain a year before. As I sat in the church, I lit a candle in her memory. As evening arrived, the swallows began their darting flights. I sat watching them dive and turn above the cobblestone street and smiled.

Saying Goodbye

It was the 24th day of walking the Camino, and as with most mornings, it was a dark start to the day as we followed the faint yellow arrows painted on the stone walls of Rabanal. Sunrise started with streaks of pink and whispery high clouds that formed a blanket of color overhead. The terrain continued to get more wooded, and in the distance, the hills had grown in height and still carried snow near their summits. With the sun, more details of the hills emerged and they were covered in purple. I assumed it was the same purple heather that grew along our path.

The countryside just got more magnificent. The first village we passed through was Foncebadon which seemed abandoned with many of the stone buildings collapsed and in disrepair. The path continued to climb to the highest point of the Camino at 4,937 feet. Tim and I entered some trees and as we came around a corner, we encountered a couple selling freshly picked cherries. They handed us a sample of the deep red fruit and it wasn't ten paces before we turned around and each of us a purchased a small bag. The cherries' sweetness distracted my mind from my tired feet.

As we approached our high point and the important stop at La Cruz de Ferro (the Iron Cross), the trail was lined with yellow and white scotch broom and the hills in the distance were covered in dark purple heather. Tradition has it that a pilgrim leaves a stone from their home at the base of the cross. The mound of stones left by thousands of pilgrims throughout the years is quite impressive. I had carried a small stone from my backyard in the States and had inscribed the names of Doris Hood, Suzanne Allen, Elmer Hood, and my two dogs Karma and Tara. All who had died over the last year. I climbed to the top of the mound and placed my stone at the cross' base and said a prayer. In a nearby field a man played a Spanish bagpipe. My eyes teared at the beauty and the somberness of the moment as I said goodbye.

Cruz de Fero

Brutal Heat

It was another lengthy day of walking and the temperatures were brutal, over 100 degrees by the afternoon. Our small group split up with Greg wanting to spend more time visiting the sites rather than the daily grind of walking every day and missing so much along the way. I didn't blame him but felt like in order to finish the 500 miles, we needed to keep on schedule.

It was four miles to Ponferrada but took over an hour to get through the town of 62,000 people. Exiting the outskirts, we entered the countryside following mostly paved roads as we powered through the 19 miles to Villafranca.

The day was fairly mundane with mile after mile of walking. At one point I had to get out of the beating sun and sat under a tree in a small park and took a long break. My ankle was bothering me and Mike had stomach issues, but other than the blisters and a short case of shin splints our bodies were holding up quite well. My wife, Beck, was scheduled to fly the next day from Seattle to New York, then on to Madrid and Santiago. I hoped all her connections would work out, that the hotel in Santiago would be available, and that the driver would get her the 60 miles to Sarria on the date we had agreed to meet. After the miserable time I had getting to Bayonne, I hoped all would go smoothly for her.

The Engineers

Our room at the alberque only had four beds and the sound of the river below an open window made the night's sleep superb. The morning started quite cool as we followed a paved road along the river for the first 11 miles of the days walking. We stopped twice for coffee. One of the cafes that overlooked the river (Rio Valcarce) had the most amazing fresh baked pastries, the highlight of the day for me. As we left the pavement, the path became a dirt trail as we started our 2,300-foot climb up into Galicia. The trees gave way to open hills. I passed two elderly women dressed all in black walking along the road. A mile or so beyond a small village appeared with a weathered stone church. We entered the dark interior and appreciated the simple house of worship. It felt more authentic than the grand cathedrals of Leon and Burges.

Our cool morning changed dramatically as the heat became oppressive. A small lavender butterfly hovered around me and I viewed it as a good omen as well as a distraction from the heat and exhaustion. Nearing the top of another ridge we encountered a large group of tourists who had been bused to the top and walked in front of us for a couple of miles where their return buses waited. I felt a bit of resentment at their fresh clean clothes and happy chattering as I stumbled along.

I don't recall how long it took to reach the mountain top village of O'Cebreiro but I was quite happy to be done. The one alberque, which had 100 beds, already had a long queue of backpacks and tired pilgrims. We waited over an hour in the sun to get registered and assigned a bed. I felt sick from the heat. Once settled, I took a nap, shower and found a small bar for an early dinner and several cold beers. Thunderstorms rolled through that evening, one after another, unleashing waterfalls from the sky. At least it was cooler.

During dinner, one of the lenses of my eye glasses fell out. The small fiberglass wire that held the bottom of the lens broke and there was nothing to hold it in place. It became a crisis as I could not see very well without them. Mike and Tim, both engineers, embraced it as a project. They took my clip-on sunglasses and with a little duct tape were able to attach the lens, at least temporarily. The only problem was that I had to wear the sunglass lenses and as night approached it was a bit difficult to see.

Galicia

Old Dog

It was quite a feat to begin the days walk, in the dark, with sunglasses. Luckily, we started down a paved road with a white stripe painted down the middle that I was able to follow until the sun began to rise. I felt pretty silly with my new eye wear but the clip-on sunglasses were the only thing holding my glasses together.

The scenery had changed to serene pastures with small rectangular storage sheds on stilts. They were designed to keep the corn and grain safe from rodents. As we were now in the province of Galicia, there were many ups and downs over the hills making the day more difficult than anticipated. We passed through a number of small villages where the stone roads were covered in manure. The smell and slickness were somewhat of a challenge. I walked past several locals herding cattle along the road. Many used trios of dogs in varying sizes and breeds who seem to love keeping the cattle in a tight group and moving forward. There was an old German Shepherd who moved so slowly that I felt sorry for him but he was committed to doing his duty as he had done for his long hard life, a life with purpose.

Glue, Ingenuity and Pasta

The day's thirteen-mile walk went rather quickly and we were able to get lodging in a small private alberque with a full kitchen and a grocery store next door. We purchased salami, bread, cheese, red sauce, pasta and several bottles of red wine and the two engineers set to work on repairing my glasses while our dinner simmered. They were able to fix them with some glue and ingenuity. The repair worked quite well though they were not very stylish. I was able to phone Beck and she made it to Santiago. Everything was going according to plan for us to meet up in Sarria where she would join in walking the last 60 miles to Santiago.

Hobbit World

The morning was busy with a large number of pilgrims getting an early start. We walked in semi darkness up a dirt path to the top of a rise with views of misty valleys and clouds hanging over damp fields and stands of trees. Once we started down the other side, the path turned into a tunnel with a dry polished streambed underfoot and a canopy of flowering trees and vines overhead. It was a damp hobbit world that I relished.

We only had eleven miles to reach Sarria and easily found the hotel where I would meet Beck. I checked into my room and went with Mike and Tim up the street where they secured a bed in one of the many alberques in Sarria. I went back to my room and took an amazing bath. Before I settled in the phone rang and Mike and Tim who were downstairs in the lobby. I joined them and we went to the cafeteria and drank mugs of hard apple cider. Beck arrived from Santiago by taxi. I was so pleased to see her. She dropped off her backpack and we took a walk by the river, sitting on a bench and talking. It had been over a month since I left home. I looked forward to having her by my side as we walked the last of the Camino to Santiago.

Fairies Live Here

Beck and I were awake by 5:00 AM and met Tim and Mike in front of their alberque under a full white moon as we exited town in the darkness. We had 14 miles of walking mostly through woods, farmland and lush greenery. Beck found the countryside magical as the sun rose and a mist hovered just above the fields making the velvety scenery mysterious. There was one section that was lined with huge ancient trees and the morning sun filtered through the leaves and branches, with sparkling specks of light. Beck stopped and with a smile whispered "Fairies live here."

Tim and Mike pulled ahead before long and after of few hours of walking stopped and waited for us at a cafe in the village of Morgade. We had a delicious breakfast of eggs, ham and bread along with a couple cups of espresso. Really the first full breakfast we had had on the Camino and a welcome treat for Beck's first day. We arrived in Portomarin in six hours. As we approached the town a long bridge crossed a waterway, Embalse de Belesar, and at the opposite end a steep section of steps took us to the towns entrance gate. The day had turned very hot and we rested under a bus stop to get out of the heat and get oriented to the town map that was in the small guide book I had carried since France. After some wandering, we found the main square and our pre-booked pension/hotel room. I had found a small travel company based in Santiago online prior to leaving the States and had them book small rooms for the six remaining nights of walking to Santiago. I didn't want to spend the last few nights in the communal alberques after not seeing Beck for over a month. I had become tired of the bunk bed dormitories.

When we found our pension, the front desk did not have our

name in the handwritten reservation ledger. After calming myself down I was able to call the agency who responded quickly and it was easily solved (the clerk had not turned over the page in the ledger to the current day). We checked into our room, met Tim and Mike for lunch, and spent the rest of the day relaxing. The day was a good start for Beck's pilgrimage to Santiago. She did an awesome job and I told her how proud I was of her. It has been a long road for her to get her strength and confidence back after her cancer. She is so excited and had trained every day for months to be able to join me on one of my adventures. I knew she would be able to finish the 60 miles to Santiago and looked forward to sharing that moment with her when it ended in front of the cathedral.

Fairies

Short Roping

We awoke at 5:00 and I taped Beck's feet as she had the start of a couple of blisters after the prior day's walk. We met up with Tim and Mike under a lamp on a dark street in front of their alberque. The day would be the last day of walking as a group as they planned on pushing fast to the end while Beck and I would take an extra day to break up the mileage. It was 15 miles of walking with the first half mostly uphill. Beck was slow and steady with all the climbing we had to do. She did very well. On the steeper sections I would take her hand and walk/pull her along until we got to the top of the rise, my version of what climbers call "short roping." The scenery was not as magical as the day before but still delightful with the highlight of the day walking through a stand of huge towering trees that formed a cathedral canopy of foliage. The weather had changed and it was cooler and rain was imminent. Our hotel was about a quarter mile before the actual town of Palas de Rei and we were able to get settled in our room before the weather took a turn for the worse. We found a small bar and sipped wine while a downpour pelted the streets. We ended up walking back to our hotel in the rain but not minding it so much after a drink or two. The rest of the evening was spent on the deck at the hotel enjoying a great meal, some very nice red wine and the Spanish rain.

No Pulpo

We had gone to bed early the night before so had plenty of sleep and only eight miles of walking to get to Melinde. It was a rough start this morning as Beck had a sharp pain in her ankle and kept having to stop and retie her boot laces. I pulled out the athletic tape and was able to tape her ankle and that seemed to do the trick. The morning was cool and cloudy with the path passing through one small hamlet after another. Many more pilgrims were walking this last stretch of the Camino as you can still get your Compostela if you walk the last 60 miles.

We arrived in Melinde around 11:00 AM and easily found our hotel, Carlos 96. I tried to use my basic Spanish to check-in, only to find that the front desk attendant was a Brit who spoke perfect English. He thankfully quickly cut short my poor attempt at Spanish conversation. We had a beer, got our room and quickly headed to the main square to find a pharmacy to purchase more tape for Beck's feet. It was still before the 2:00 PM siesta so we found a restaurant to try the local dish of boiled octopus (pulpo a la Gallega). The small chunks of chewy pungent meat served on a wooden plate was not what we expected, and not to be repeated.

The rain and wind pounded against the windows all night. I had planned for us to get an early start but with the nasty weather it didn't make sense. The rain was torrential. I lay in the darkness torn between waking and exiting into the storm, or staying in the warm bed with the hope that it would lighten up. I have always enjoyed the tempest. To find a small shelter and watch the wind whip the trees and hear its roar is one of my favorite things.

Two Bottles of Rioja

We only had eight miles to walk for the day so we stayed in bed until after sunrise and left the room a little after 7:00 AM. It was lightly raining and the wind had dropped down to just some occasional heavy gusts. We had a short walk out of town though Beck wasn't feeling too well, since our octopus dinner had made her sick in the night. Once we entered the woods on the outskirts of town the path was mostly dirt through a grove of fragrant eucalyptus trees, such a wonderful smell in the morning dampness. We were ahead of the hordes of pilgrims so were able to walk most of the day alone. A small village cafe was open and we took our time and enjoyed the rest as it was only a couple hours more before we arrived in Ribadiso and our pension. Luckily, we only had about a half hour of rain just before we arrived in town. We each took a nice hot shower, that removed the day's damp chill, and took a short nap. Towards evening we found a small cafe with a wonderful, sweet family who made us feel welcome. Greg arrived in town and joined us after almost a week of not seeing him and the three of us caught up on conversation over two amazing bottles of Rioja to end the evening.

Vineyard House

Missing the Solitude

We walked fourteen miles to Pedrouza the next day over rolling hills of oak and eucalyptus forests. Small villages and hamlets were strung together, tied by the wandering yellow arrows of the Camino. There were lots of wild flowers along the path and the usual bird chorus in the early morning fog. The moon was waning. The first few hours provided solitude but before long large numbers of pilgrims began to catch up with us. The prior weeks had provided so much solitude and I missed the lack of people.

We arrived in Pedrouza after five hours and enjoyed a cold beer at a small cafe until our hotel opened. The rest of the day was spent relaxing. The next day would be the last day of walking. After 34 days I had walked the whole Camino de Santiago. I hadn't been sure I could accomplish it and being so close to the end had me anxious. The day-to-day routine and the time alone with my thoughts had been a beautiful pause in my life.

The Last Day

I didn't sleep very well and began looking at my watch shortly after midnight as I wanted us to be walking as early as possible on this the last day of the Camino. I awoke at 4:00 AM and laid in bed just gazing into the dark until 5:00. We got up and I retaped Beck's feet for the last time. We headed out into the dark past several very drunk Spanish teenagers staggering down the street after the early morning bar closures. We had a difficult time finding the Camino signs, but thankfully Greg appeared with two other pilgrims and as a group we were able to find the yellow arrow that led from the town down a very dark forest path. All of us had headlamps or flashlights and we stumbled along in the almost pitch blackness. Beck and I were slower than the rest and eventually we lost track of the others.

Eventually we made the steady climb up to Monte Gozo, Hill of Joy. From Monte Gozo we could see Santiago and the end of the Camino. As we headed down a huge relief came over me and even though it began to rain my mood was joyous. Santiago's outskirts seemed to stretch on forever. It took a long time to finally reach the old city gate and the main square. We entered the square and stood in front of the massive cathedral of Santiago. I leaned on my walking staff and took a deep breath. Emotions hit me and I stood in the rain with tears running down my face. Beck reached over and held my hand.

As we climbed the stone steps, I gave a begging woman some coins and entered the cathedral where we found an empty pew towards the back. We waited for an hour before the noon mass and pilgrims who I had seen and had gotten to know over the past month began to arrive. David, a young Spaniard, who had walked from France as well, stopped by and said hello. The mass began with a nun who sang praise with a voice that filled the cathedral with a beautiful sound. A young woman sitting next to us knelt and cried as she prayed. All around us were the devout. This trip was an amazing emotional ride. I become overwhelmed and cried so many times: in the small hamlet churches, at the cross of rocks, thinking of family and friends who have died, and in front of the cathedral here in Santiago at the end of the walking; tired, cold and finished. I had come closer to my personal God whom I thanked.

After the Pilgrim's Mass we walked to the Office of Pilgrims to get our "Compostela". The line was extremely long but we were patient and with the documents in hand we exited the building. Tim and Mike were a welcome surprise standing outside waiting for us. We hugged and congratulated one another and headed to a small cafe and enjoyed a glass of wine. Afterwards the two of them walked us to our hotel.

We spent the evening with Mike, Tim, Greg and a Canadian woman whom we had met a few weeks prior, telling stories of the Camino. Tim shared that I had persisted in calling a local soda Aqua Reese, my Spanish translation of Aquarius. Another "Kim-ism." We found a bar that specialized in absinthe and made the mistake of doing an extensive tasting. Beck and I ended up sitting against a wall in a square laughing and wondering how Mike and Tim were going to make it back to their hotel room and catch an early morning flight home to the States.

Incense

Sunday was our last day in Santiago. When we attended the Pilgrim's Mass the day before, the service had not included the swinging of the huge incense burner or thurible. Since we had one more day in Santiago, we decided to attend another Mass. This time we were treated to the spectacle. Six burgundy robed attendants gathered around a series of ropes and pulled, lifting the huge metal container (Botafumeiro) upwards. With each pull the massive smoking incense burner began to swing across the width of the cathedral. The sun filtered through the smoke as it swirled upwards until broken by the next swing of the burner. I sat enthralled.

Heading Home

After a few more days in Spain, we were on the flight home. It seemed like I had been gone a very long time. Walking the Camino provided so much insight into my life. The simplicity of the daily routine of just walking all day allowed so much time for reflection. The walk had many emotional moments, and I was glad to have shared the last miles with Beck.

Rabanal del Camino

Conclusion

My friend Tim and I reflected that on completing these three pilgrimages, we had walked with those who believe in various paths to God. Through Buddhism, Hinduism, Islam and Christianity. We agreed we saw the very best of humanity. For me, it confirmed my belief in the spiritual connection between people and a God. I joked to Tim, who was a non-believer, that even though he might not put much credence in "all that spiritual stuff", the pilgrimages couldn't hurt, just in case.

Author

KIM EUGENE HOOD studied fine art and graduated from the University of Washington. After years in the corporate world, he rediscovered his art. He graduated from the Photographic Center Northwest in Seattle Washington with a certificate in fine art photography. Kim was an outdoor guide and currently is a fine art photographer. His passion for travel and exploration has driven him to climb and trek in mountain ranges on all seven continents. Over the last thirty years he has visited dozens of spiritual and religious sites worldwide and completed the religious pilgrimages of the Hindu Char Dham in northern India, the Buddhist kora around Mt. Kailash and the Catholic Camino de Santiago in northern Spain.